3

AVENUES
English Grammar

Lynne Gaetz

TEACHER'S ANNOTATED EDITION

PEARSON

Montréal

Managing Editor
Sharnee Chait

Editor
Lucie Turcotte

Copy Editor
Stacey Berman

Proofreader
Katie Moore

Coordination, Rights and Permissions
Pierre Richard Bernier

Art Director
Hélène Cousineau

Graphic Design Coordinator
Lyse LeBlanc

Book Design and Layout
Interscript

Cover Design
Frédérique Bouvier

Cover Artwork
Pietro Adamo, *Citta Series*, 2009. Mixed media on paper, 36 x 24 inches. Courtesy of Progressive Fine Art and Galerie Beauchamp. © 2011 Artist Pietro Adamo.

ERPI publishes and distributes PEARSON ELT products in Canada.

5757 Cypihot Street
Saint-Laurent, Québec H4S 1R3
CANADA
Telephone: 1 800 263-3678
Fax: 1 866 334-0448
infoesl@pearsonerpi.com
http://pearsonelt.ca

Registration of copyright – Bibliothèque et Archives nationales du Québec, 2013
Registration of copyright – Library and Archives Canada, 2013

Printed in Canada 123456789 II 17 16 15 14 13
ISBN 978-2-7613-5122-5 135122 ABCD ENV94

Acknowledgements

Many people helped produce what you hold in your hands. I would like to express sincere thanks to

- Sharnee Chait for her valuable expertise;
- Lucie Turcotte for her patience and insight while editing this book;
- Julie Hough for her enthusiasm, which helped ignite this project;
- My students at Collège Lionel-Groulx for their insightful feedback;
- Diego Pelaez for his valuable contributions to this manuscript and the Companion Website;
- Interscript for the creative layout.

Finally, I dedicate this to my children Diego and Rebeka.

100 %
BIO GAS ENERGY
MIX
Paper from responsible sources
FSC www.fsc.org FSC® C011825

This book is printed on paper made in Québec from 100% post-consumer recycled materials, processed chlorine-free, certified Eco-Logo, and manufactured using biogas energy.

3

AVENUES

Grammar Review Guide

Lynne Gaetz

Contents

123456789 IO 17 16 15 14 13
135123 ENV94

135123
ISBN 978-2-7613-5123-2
9 782761 351232

IMPRIMÉ AU CANADA PRINTED IN CANADA

ELT

PEARSON

ALWAYS LEARNING

1. Adjectives and Adverbs

Adjectives modify a noun and generally appear before the noun. Adjectives are always singular, even if the nouns they modify are plural.

We admired the **sleek tall** buildings.

Adverbs give information about a verb. Most adverbs end in *–ly*. Some exceptions are the adverbs *fast*, *high*, *far*, *late*, *often*, and *soon*, which never end in *–ly*.

Liam played the piano **quickly**. (The adverb *quickly* describes the action of playing.)

COMPARATIVE AND SUPERLATIVE FORMS OF ADJECTIVES AND ADVERBS

	ADJECTIVE OR ADVERB	COMPARATIVE	SUPERLATIVE
Add *–er* or *–est* to one-syllable adjectives. When the adjective ends in a consonant-vowel-consonant, double the last letter.	short fast hot	short**er than** fast**er than** hot**ter than**	**the** short**est** **the** fast**est** **the** hot**test**
In two-syllable adjectives ending in a consonant + *–y*, change *–y* to *–i* and add *–er* (comparative form) or *–est* (superlative form).	easy funny	eas**ier than** funn**ier than**	**the** eas**iest** **the** funn**iest**
Add *more* (comparative form) or *the most* (superlative form) to adjectives of two or more syllables and to compound adjectives.	modern well-liked	**more** modern **than** **more** well-liked **than**	**the most** modern **the most** well-liked
Add *more* (comparative form) or *the most* (superlative form) to adverbs ending in *–ly*.	easily quickly	**more** easily **than** **more** quickly **than**	**the most** easily **the most** quickly
Some adjectives and adverbs have special comparative and superlative forms.	good/well bad/badly much/many little (small amount) far	**better than** **worse than** **more than** **less than** **farther than**	**the best** **the worst** **the most** **the least** **the farthest/ the furthest**

EQUALITY: AS ... AS/THE SAME AS

Both *as ... as* and *the same as* express equality.

Ray is **as guilty as** his brother. My cellphone is **the same as** yours.

FREQUENCY ADVERBS

Adverbs modify verbs and can express time or frequency. Place frequency adverbs

- after *be* — I **am** **often** tired. He **is** **rarely** late.
- before all other simple tense verbs — He **usually** **walks** to work.
- after an auxiliary verb — She **can** **always** **help** you.
- after the subject in question forms — Does **she** **sometimes** work too hard?

2. Capitalization

Always capitalize

- the pronoun *I* and the first word of every sentence

    The man that **I** met is very nice.

- the days of the week, the months, and holidays

    Friday | **J**une 8 | **L**abour **D**ay

- the names of specific places, such as buildings, streets, parks, public squares, lakes, rivers, cities, provinces, and countries

    Evan **A**venue | **L**ake Erie | **C**algary, **A**lberta

- the names of languages, nationalities, tribes, races, and religions

    Spanish | **M**ohawk | **P**rotestant

- the titles of specific individuals

    General **D**allaire | **P**rime **M**inister **L**ee | **M**rs. **P**eel

- the titles of specific courses

    Physics 201 | **E**nglish 101 | **B**eginner's **S**panish

- certain historical events, eras, and movements

    World **W**ar II | **C**ubism | **G**roup of **S**even

- the important words in titles of literary or artistic works

    ***S**ource **C**ode* | ***M**odern **F**amily* | ***B**ad **R**omance*

3. Combining Sentences

You can combine sentences in a variety of ways.

COORDINATORS AND SUBORDINATORS

Inside sentences, you can connect ideas with **coordinators** (*and*, *but*, *so*, *or*, *yet*, *for*, *nor*).

I love the winter, **but** I don't like driving in the snow.

You can also join a secondary idea to a main idea with a **subordinator** (see list below).

I love the winter **although** I hate cleaning the snow off my car.

COMMON SUBORDINATORS

TIME		REASON, CAUSE, OR EFFECT	CONDITION	CONTRAST	LOCATION
after	when	as	as long as	although	where
before	while	because	if	even though	wherever
since		since	so that	though	
until			unless	whereas	

TRANSITIONAL WORDS AND EXPRESSIONS

Use transitional words to connect sentences and paragraphs. When you use the expressions listed in the chart on page 4, put a comma after the expression.

First, some people drive too fast.

COMMON TRANSITIONAL WORDS AND EXPRESSIONS

CHRONOLOGY (Sequence of ideas)	COMPARISON AND CONTRAST	ADDITIONAL ARGUMENT	EXAMPLE	EMPHASIS	SUMMARY OR CONCLUSION
after that currently eventually finally first, second, third* formerly in the meantime later meanwhile next suddenly then	conversely equally however in contrast in the same way instead nevertheless on the contrary on the one hand on the other hand similarly	additionally also as well besides furthermore in addition moreover	for example for instance in fact in particular namely specifically to illustrate	above all certainly clearly definitely in fact in particular indeed more importantly of course principally specifically undoubtedly	as a result consequently evidently finally hence in conclusion in other words in short on the whole therefore/thus to conclude to sum up

* Do not write *firstly, secondly, thirdly*. It is preferable to write *first, second, third*.

4. Conditionals

Conditional sentences have two parts. The main clause depends on the condition set in the *if*-clause.

***If*-clause (the condition)**	**the result**
If we work hard,	we will finish the project.

POSSIBLE PRESENT AND FUTURE

In these sentences, the condition is true or very possible.

***If* + present tense**	**present or future tense**
If you **think** about it,	life **is** pretty great. (This present situation is true.)
If you **study,**	you **will** pass the course. (This will probably happen.)

UNLIKELY PRESENT

In these sentences, the condition is something that is very improbable or impossible.

***If* + past tense**	***would* (expresses an intention)** ***could* (expresses a possibility)**
If I **won** a million dollars in the lottery,	I **would buy** a new car.

In the *if*-clause, the past verb tense is used. With the verb *be*, the *were* form is used with all subjects. (In colloquial, or "street" English, you will occasionally hear *was*.)

If I **were** you, I **would stop** complaining.

IMPOSSIBLE PAST

In impossible past sentences, the condition is something that can't happen because the event is over. The speaker expresses regret about a past event or a wish that a past event had worked out differently.

***If* + past perfect tense**	***would have* + past participle**
If you **had completed** your assignment,	you **would have passed** the course.

USING *WISH*

Wish about the present

You make a wish when you want things to be different. When you wish about a present situation, use the past tense. With the verb *to be*, always use *were* in formal English.

I wish I **knew** how to play the violin. (I can't play the violin, but I would like to.)

He wishes that he **were** stronger.

Wish about the past

When you wish you could change a past situation, use the past perfect tense.

Leo wishes that he **had told** the truth to his wife.

5. Determiners

A and ***an*** mean "one." Only put *a* or *an* before singular count nouns.

- Use *a* before nouns that begin with a consonant. — **a** friend, **a** house
  - **Exception:** When *u* sounds like "you" put *a* before it. — **a** union
- Use *an* before nouns that begin with a vowel. — **an** apple, **an** umbrella
  - **Exception:** Use *an* before words that begin with a silent *h*. — **an** honest man, **an** hour

Use ***the*** to indicate a specific noun (or specific nouns). *The* can be placed before singular or plural nouns.

I need to find **a** (general) new shirt. **The** (specific) shirts in that store are expensive.

DETERMINERS WITH COUNT AND NONCOUNT NOUNS

COUNT NOUNS (*many, few, a few*)	NONCOUNT NOUNS (*much, little, a little*)	COUNT AND NONCOUNT NOUNS (*a lot of*)
She has **very few*** friends. She has **a few**** friends. He has **many** friends.	She has **very little*** money. She has **a little**** money. He doesn't have **much***** money.	He has **a lot of***** friends and **a lot of** money.

* *Few* and *little* mean "almost none" and often indicate complaints.
** *A few* and *a little* mean "a small amount." There is no negative connotation.
*** Use *much* only in negative and question forms. In affirmative forms, use *a lot of* instead.

6. Modals

COMMON MODAL AUXILIARIES			
FUNCTION	**MODAL**	**EXAMPLE**	**PAST FORM**
ability	**can**	I **can climb** mountains.	**could climb**
polite request (question form)	**may** **would** **could** **can**	**May** I **help** you? (formal) **Would** you **like** some coffee? **Could** you **open** the door? **Can** I **help** you? (informal)	
advice opinion	**should** **ought to**	She **should see** a lawyer. The lawyer **ought to see** her.	**should have seen** **ought to have seen**

➜

obligation	**must** **have to***	Now, the baby **must sleep**. Now, she **has to sleep**.	**had to sleep** (past form of both *must* and *have to*)
probability	**must**	Chantal **must be** tired.	**must have been**
possibility	**could** **might** **may**	The clerk **could help** you. I **might take** the job. Ann **may need** them.	**could have helped** **might have taken** **may have needed**
condition desire preference past habit	**would** **would like** **would rather**	If I had time, I **would visit** her. (expresses a wish) I **would like** some coffee. I **would rather be** happy than rich. In my youth, I **would drive** for hours.	**would have visited** **would have liked** **would rather have been**

*Although *have to* isn't a modal auxiliary, it is included on this list because it functions like a modal and has the same meaning as *must*. For question and negative forms, you must add *do* or *does*.

Does he have to leave? He doesn't have to leave.

Note: *Gotta* is often heard in spoken English, but it should never be written. It is really an incorrect contraction of *got* and *to*. Make a habit of using *have to* instead of *got to* or *gotta*.

have to
I ~~gotta~~ find a job.

7. Nouns

A **noun** is a word that refers to a person, place, or thing. A **count noun** refers to a person, place, or thing that can be counted and has a plural form. A **noncount noun** refers to something that cannot be counted and has only a singular form. Often, noncount nouns refer to categories of objects or abstract concepts.

We had a lot of **homework**. (noncount noun)   We have three **assignments**. (count noun)

NONCOUNT NOUNS

Here are some common noncount nouns. They have no plural form.

CATEGORIES OF OBJECTS		FOOD	NATURE AND SUBSTANCES	ABSTRACT NOUNS	
baggage	machinery	bread	air	advice	knowledge
clothing	mail	cheese	chalk	attention	luck
equipment	makeup	fish	coal	behaviour	patience
furniture	money	honey	electricity	education	publicity
homework	music	meat	fur	effort	proof
housework	postage	milk	hair	evidence	research
ink	software	rice	paint	health	time**
jewellery	wildlife	salt	radiation	help	trouble
luggage	work*	sugar	weather	information	violence

* *Work* is a noncount noun except when it refers to artistic works.
** *Time* is a noncount noun when it refers to free time or spare time.

PLURAL FORMS

Many English nouns have irregular plural forms.

man ▶ **men**   child ▶ **children**   tooth ▶ **teeth**   mouse ▶ **mice**
woman ▶ **women**   person ▶ **people**   foot ▶ **feet**   sheep ▶ **sheep**

Most nouns that end in *–f* or *–fe* change to *–ves* in the plural form. (**Exception:** belief ▶ beliefs)

life ▶ **lives**   scarf ▶ **scarves**   shelf ▶ **shelves**   thief ▶ **thieves**

8. Phrasal Verbs

A phrasal verb, which consists of a verb and preposition, forms a single idea. Here are some commonly used phrasal verbs.

PHRASAL VERB	MEANING	PHRASAL VERB	MEANING
act up	– to act improperly	find out	– to discover
add up	– to calculate	fool around	– to waste time
back up	– to move in reverse – to support; to make protective copies (computer term)	freak out	– to overreact
blow up	– to explode or inflate	get by	– to survive financially
bone up	– to study	get ready	– to prepare
break down	– to stop working – to collapse emotionally	give away	– to give something for free
break in	– to use force to enter a locked place	give up	– to surrender – to stop a habit (give up alcohol)
break up	– to end a relationship	grow up	– to mature
bring up	– to introduce a subject	hand in	– to submit work to someone
brush up	– to practise	hang out	– to spend time with someone
butt in	– to interrupt	hang up	– to end a phone conversation
butter up	– to praise excessively; to flatter	hurry up	– to go faster
call back	– to return a phone call	lay off	– to temporarily dismiss an employee
call off	– to cancel	look after	– to take care of
call up	– to phone someone	make out	– to identify with difficulty – to kiss and touch
carry on	– to continue	make up	– to reunite after a fight
catch on	– to become popular	move over	– to move to the side
check in	– to register at a hotel	pass out	– to distribute – to lose consciousness
chip in	– to contribute	put off	– to postpone
clam up	– to stop talking	rip off	– to steal
close down	– to close permanently	run away	– to secretly leave (home}
close up	– to close temporarily	take after	– to resemble
cross out	– to make an X over something	take back	– to retrieve
cut back	– to reduce the use of something	take off	– to remove (clothing) – to leave
dress up	– to wear formal clothing	take over	– to gain control of something
drop off	– to fall asleep – to leave someone or deliver something somewhere – to decline	throw away	– to put in the garbage
drop out	– to quit school	turn off	– to stop a machine or light
figure out	– to solve	turn on	– to start a machine or light
fill in/out	– to complete a form	try on	– to wear something to see if it fits

9. Prepositions

IN, *ON*, AND *AT*

Use ***in***, ***on***, and ***at*** as follows:

In a year, month, city, country, continent

In March, **in** 2012, we stayed **in** London.

On a day of the week, a specific date, a specific street

On March 2, **on** Tuesday, **on** Main Street, we saw a fight.

At a specific time of day, a specific address

At 11:00 **at** night, we stayed **at** a hotel.

FOR AND *DURING*

Both *for* and *during* indicate that an activity happened over a period of time. However, these words aren't interchangeable. Use *during* to explain when something happened. Use *for* to explain how long it took to happen.

The restaurant closed **for** two hours **during** the blackout.

During the strike, the hotel workers protested **for** six hours.

PREPOSITIONAL EXPRESSIONS

Many nouns, verbs, and adverbs are followed by certain prepositions.

accuse (somebody) of
acquainted with
add to
afraid of
agree with
angry with/about
apologize for
apply for
approve of
argue with
ask for
associate with
aware of
believe in
belong to
capable of
care about/for
commit to
comply with
concern about
confronted with
consist of
count on
deal with
decide to/on
depend on
disappointed with/about
dream of
escape from
excited about
familiar with
feel like
fond of
forget about
forgive (someone) for
friendly with
good for
grateful for
happy about
hear about/of
hope for
hopeful about
insist on
insulted by
interested in
interfere with
introduce to
jealous of
keep from
located in
long for
look forward to
opposed to
participate in
patient with
pay attention to
pay for
pray for
prepared for
prevent (someone) from
protect (someone) from
proud of
provide (someone) with
qualify for
realistic about
refer to
related to
rely on
rescue from
responsible for
sad about
satisfied with
scared of
search for
similar to
specialize in
stop (something) from
succeed in
take advantage of
take care of
thank (someone) for
think about/of
tired of
upset with/about
willing to
wish for
worry about

10. Pronouns

	SUBJECT PRONOUNS replace the subject and are generally followed by a verb. **She** lives alone.	**OBJECT PRONOUNS** replace the object and are usually found after a verb or preposition. I saw **him** yesterday.	**POSSESSIVE ADJECTIVES** describe a noun and appear before the noun that they describe. That is **our** house.	**POSSESSIVE PRONOUNS** indicate possession and replace a noun. That house is **ours**.	**REFLEXIVE PRONOUNS** reflect back on the subject. The child can feed **herself**.
Singular	I you he she it	me you him her it	my your his her its	mine yours his hers —	myself yourself himself herself itself
Plural	we you they	us you them	our your their	ours yours theirs	ourselves yourselves themselves

INDEFINITE PRONOUNS

When the antecedent is a singular indefinite pronoun such as *everybody*, *something*, or *nobody*, use a singular pronoun to refer to it. If the gender of the subject is unknown, or if the subjects include both genders, use both the male and female pronouns. If the sentence then appears awkward, simply change the subject to a plural noun.

Incorrect: Everybody must submit **their** answers to the professor.

Solution: Everybody must submit **his or her** answers to the professor.

Better solution: The students must submit **their** answers to the professor.

PRONOUNS AFTER *OR*

When the nouns are joined by *or* or *nor*, the pronoun form is the same as the form of the noun that is nearest to it.

singular form

Does either Milgram or Zimbardo have regrets about **his** experiment?

PRONOUNS AFTER *ONE OF THE/EACH OF THE*

In a sentence containing the expression *one of the* or *each of the*, the subject is the indefinite pronoun *one* or *each*. You must use a singular pronoun to refer to the subject.

One of the women spoke with **her** lawyer.

PRONOUNS IN COMPARISONS

When a pronoun follows a comparison that uses *than* or *as*, ensure that you use the correct pronoun. To verify that your pronoun is correct, complete the thought.

I like psychology better than (**he** or **him**).

Complete the thought: I like psychology better than **he** (**likes psychology**).

SUBJECT PRONOUN OR OBJECT PRONOUN?

When a pronoun is paired with a noun, the correct choice of pronoun isn't always obvious. A simple way to determine the correct pronoun is to say the sentence with just that pronoun.

The professor asked Martin and (**I** or **me**) to present our topic.

Possible choices: The professor asked **I**./The professor asked **me**.

Correct answer: The professor asked Martin and **me** to present our topic.

11. Punctuation

APOSTROPHES (')

Use apostrophes

- to join a subject and verb together — **We're** late.
- to join an auxiliary with *not* — I **can't** come.
- to indicate possession — **Ross's** computer is new.
  (plural: add ') — The **girls'** school is closed.
  (irregular plural: add 's) — The **men's** room is nearby.

COLONS (:)

Use a colon

- after a complete sentence that introduces a list, or after *the following*
  The course has the following sections**:** crime, law, and justice.
- after a complete sentence that introduces a quotation
  Picasso's advice was clear**:** "Find your passion."
- to introduce an explanation or example
  I decided to confess**:** my fingerprints were at the crime scene.
- to separate the hours and minutes in expressions of time
  The store closed at 12**:**30 and reopened at 2**:**00.

COMMAS (,)

Use commas

- to separate three or more words in a series (Put the comma before the final *and*.)
  The doctor is tall**,** thin**,** and gentle.
- after an introductory word, phrase, or idea
  First**,** Mr. Chen closed his store.
  A few minutes later**,** he emptied the safe.
- around interrupting phrases that give additional information about the subject.
  Kevin**,** a student at Victoria College**,** went through a traffic light.

HYPHENS (-)

Use hyphens

- when you write the complete word for a compound number between 21 and 99
  twenty-five — ninety-two — seventy-seven
- after some prefixes, such as *ex-*, *mid-*, and *self-*
  ex-husband — mid-December — self-assured
- with some compound nouns (note that *compound* means "more than one part")
  mother-in-law — show-off — sister-in-law
- when you use a compound adjective before a noun. The compound adjective must express a single thought.
  one-way street — thirty-year-old woman — well-known actor

PERIODS (.)

Use a period

- at the end of a complete sentence
- after the following titles: *Ms.*, *Mrs.*, *Mr.*, and *Dr.* (Don't put a period after *Miss*.)

QUOTATION MARKS (" ")

Use quotation marks around direct speech.

Begin a quotation with a capital letter. Put the final comma or period inside the quotation marks.

He said**, "T**he light was green**."** **OR** **"T**he light was green**,"** he said.

- Put a comma after an introductory phrase.

Jacob shouted**, "H**elp me**!"**

- Put a colon after an introductory sentence.

The doctor delivered the news**: "Y**ou're healthy**."**

- When quotations are integrated into sentences, just put quotation marks.

Dorothy called herself a **"**terrible mother**."**

- When a quotation is inside another quotation, use single quotation marks.

Dante said, "My mother told me**, '**Don't be a comedian.**'**"

- Put the page number in parentheses after a quotation. Put the period after the parentheses.

Jan Wong said, "May God forgive me; I don't think they ever will" **(124).**

SEMICOLONS (;)

Use a semicolon to join two independent and related clauses.

Gandhi was a pacifist**;** he believed in non-violence.

12. Spelling

SOME COMMONLY MISSPELLED WORDS

absence	beginning	courteous	exercise	independence
accessible	believe	criticism	family	initiative
accidentally	benefit	deceive	finally	interesting
accommodate	between	definitely	financially	interrupt
accomplish	business	description	forty	jealousy
accumulate	calendar	developed	fourth	judge
acquaintance	career	discipline	fulfill	knowledge
address	careful	dilemma	function	language
advice (noun)	changeable	disappearance	future	leisure
advise (verb)	character	disappoint	generally	length
alcohol	commitment	dissatisfied	genius	lightning
another	company	disease	government	loneliness
apartment	completely	easily	happiness	loose (not tight)
appearance	conflict	eighth	height	lose (can't find)
appointment	conscience	embarrassed	heroes	magazine
balloon	conscientious	encouragement	historical	maintenance
bargain	continue	environment	human	manageable
basically	counsellor	exaggerate	immediately	marriage

→

medicine	occasionally	potential	really	statistics
mentioned	occurred	practically	receive	strength
millionaire	omitted	preferred	recommend	taught
miscellaneous	organization	prejudice	responsibility	technical
mortgage	panicked	privilege	restaurant	technique
naturally	parallel	proceed	schedule	through
necessary	permitted	professor	scientific	together
necessity	personal (private)	proof (noun)	separate	tomorrow
ninety	personality	prove (verb)	severely	twelfth
ninth	personnel (staff)	psychology	similar	unique
noticeable	piece	quantity	succeed (verb)	usually
nowadays	possess	questioned	success (noun)	valuable
obstacle	potato(es)	questionnaire	surely	writing

13. Subject-Verb Agreement

In the simple present tense, verbs that follow third-person singular subjects end in -s or -es. Add -es to verbs that end in *ch, sh, s, x,* or *z*.

George fix**es** cars and trucks. He wish**es** that he had a different job.

INDEFINITE PRONOUNS

Indefinite pronouns beginning with *every, some-, any-*, and *no-* are considered singular.

Everyone **has** fears, but nobody **likes** to admit it.

THERE

In sentences beginning with *there*, the subject appears after the verb. Make sure that the subject and verb agree.

There **is** a full moon tonight. (singular subject)

There **are** some clouds in the sky. (plural subject)

INTERRUPTING PHRASES

When subjects and verbs are interrupted by another phrase, make sure that the verb agrees with the subject.

One of my best friends **lives** next door.

Interrupting phrases such *as along with* or *as well as* do not form compound subjects. The subject is before the interrupting phrase.

Mac, as well as his brother, **works** in a hospital.

SUBJECTS JOINED BY *OR*

When subjects are joined by *either ... or* or *neither ... nor*, the verb agrees with the nearest subject.

Neither Ms. Lee nor her children **watch** television.

Either those dogs or Jane **has** to go.

EXPRESSIONS OF QUANTITY

When the subject is an expression of quantity—*the majority of, one-third of, a part of, ten percent of, the rest of*—the verb agrees with the noun that follows *of*.

The majority of the shareholders **want** another president.

The majority of the audience **likes** the show.

14. This/That/These/Those

This and *these* are used to refer to people and things that are close to the speaker. *That* and *those* are used to refer to things that are distant from the speaker.

	NEAR THE SPEAKER	FAR FROM THE SPEAKER
singular	**This** shirt is mine. **This** year I turn twenty-one.	**That** city is in Poland. Remember 1955? My father was born in **that** year.
plural	**These** glasses are mine. **These** days I feel tired.	**Those** cars are driving too fast. I went to school in the 1990s. **Those** years were great.

15. Verb Tense Review

VERB TENSE CHART

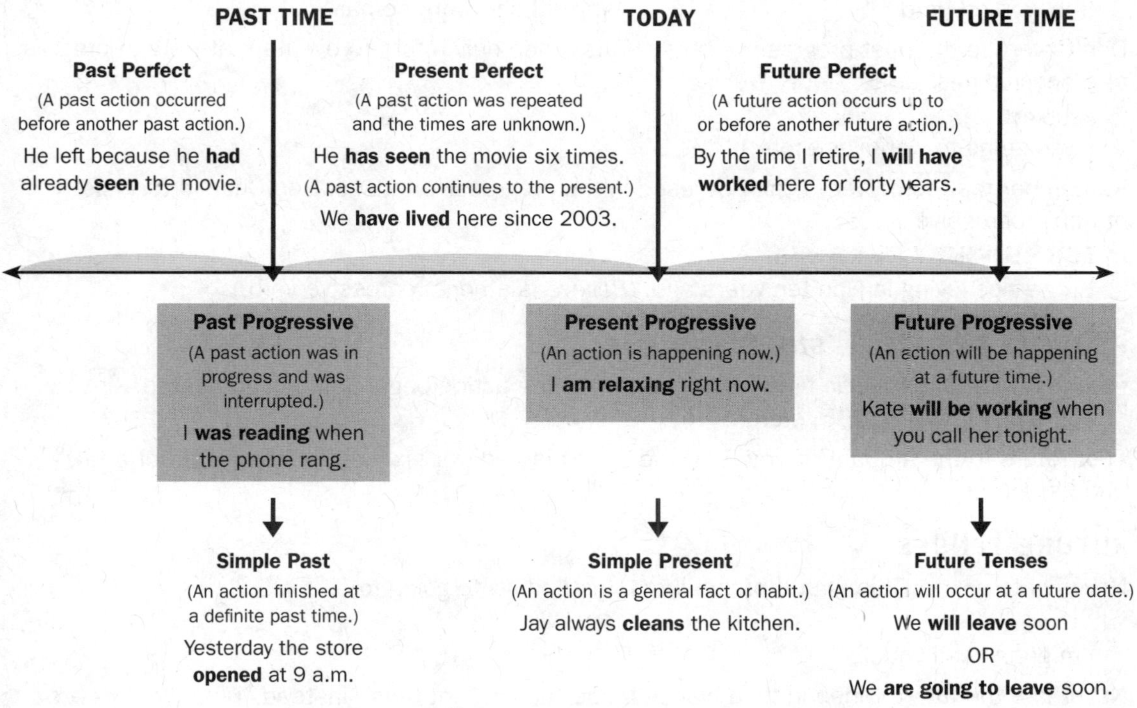

NON-PROGRESSIVE VERBS

The following verbs are generally not used in the progressive tense.

PERCEPTION	PREFERENCE	MENTAL STATE/OPINION	POSSESSION
appear & seem	dislike	believe	belong
feel	hate	know	have (meaning "possess")
hear	like	mean	own
resemble	love	recognize	possess
see	need	remember & forget	
smell	prefer	think (meaning "in my opinion")	
sound	want	understand	
taste			

PRESENT TENSES

In the simple present tense, add *do* or *does* to question and negative forms. If you add the auxiliary *does*, you must remove the -*s* from the verb.

She works hard. Why **does** she always work so hard?

Only use the present progressive tense when the action is happening now.

complains
Julie ~~is complaining~~ every day.

PAST TENSES

In simple past question and negative forms, *did* takes the past tense, and the verb reverts to its base form.

She worked hard. Why **did** she work so hard?

Don't overuse the past progressive tense. This tense only refers to events that were in progress at a specific past time.

went
I ~~was going~~ to work yesterday.

Remember that some verbs can't be used in the progressive tenses. See Chart 4 for a list of non-progressive verbs.

believed
He ~~was believing~~ in God ten years ago. (*Believe* is a non-progressive verb.)

PERFECT TENSES — *SINCE* AND *FOR*

- ***Since*** refers to a specific time in the past when the action began (since I graduated, since I was a child, since 1995, etc.).
- ***For*** refers to the amount of time that the action lasted (for six months, for years, for a few hours, etc.).

FUTURE TENSES

Never write *gonna*. This isn't a proper word. Instead, write *going to*.

going to
I'm ~~gonna~~ call you.

Never use the future tense in time clauses; use the present tense instead. Time clauses are introduced by the following time markers:

after as long as as soon as before in case until unless when while

I will call you when I **finish** work.

16. Common Irregular Verbs

BASE FORM	SIMPLE PAST	PAST PARTICIPLE	BASE FORM	SIMPLE PAST	PAST PARTICIPLE
be	was/were	been	**foresee**	foresaw	foreseen
beat	beat	beat/beaten	**forget**	forgot	forgotten
become	became	become	**forgive**	forgave	forgiven
begin	began	begun	**freeze**	froze	frozen
bend	bent	bent	**get**	got	got/gotten
bet	bet	bet	**give**	gave	given
bind	bound	bound	**go**	went	gone
bite	bit	bitten	**grind**	ground	ground
bleed	bled	bled	**grow**	grew	grown
blow	blew	blown	**hang**[1]	hung	hung
break	broke	broken	**have**	had	had
breed	bred	bred	**hear**	heard	heard
bring	brought	brought	**hide**	hid	hidden
build	built	built	**hit**	hit	hit
burst	burst	burst	**hold**	held	held
buy	bought	bought	**hurt**	hurt	hurt
catch	caught	caught	**keep**	kept	kept
choose	chose	chosen	**kneel**	knelt	knelt
cling	clung	clung	**know**	knew	known
come	came	come	**lay**	laid	laid
cost	cost	cost	**lead**	led	led
creep	crept	crept	**leave**	left	left
cut	cut	cut	**lend**	lent	lent
deal	dealt	dealt	**let**	let	let
dig	dug	dug	**lie**[2]	lay	lain
do	did	done	**light**	lit	lit
draw	drew	drawn	**lose**	lost	lost
drink	drank	drunk	**make**	made	made
drive	drove	driven	**mean**	meant	meant
eat	ate	eaten	**meet**	met	met
fall	fell	fallen	**mislead**	misled	misled
feed	fed	fed	**mistake**	mistook	mistaken
feel	felt	felt	**pay**	paid	paid
fight	fought	fought	**put**	put	put
find	found	found	**prove**	proved	proved/proven
fit	fit	fit	**quit**	quit	quit
flee	fled	fled	**read**[3]	read	read
fly	flew	flown	**ride**	rode	ridden
forbid	forbade	forbidden	**ring**	rang	rung

1. When *hang* means "to suspend by a rope, as in a form of capital punishment," then it is a regular verb. The past forms are *hanged*.
2. *Lie* means "to rest or lie down, such as on a sofa or bed." When lie means "to tell a false statement," it is a regular verb: *lie–lied–lied*.
3. The present form of *read* is pronounced "reed." The simple past and past participle forms are pronounced "red."

Continued

rise	rose	risen	**steal**	stole	stolen
run	ran	run	**stick**	stuck	stuck
say	said	said	**sting**	stung	stung
see	saw	seen	**stink**	stank	stunk
sell	sold	sold	**strike**	struck	struck
send	sent	sent	**strive**	strove	striven
set	set	set	**swear**	swore	sworn
shake	shook	shaken	**sweep**	swept	swept
shoot	shot	shot	**swim**	swam	swum
show	showed	shown	**swing**	swung	swung
shrink	shrank	shrunk	**take**	took	taken
shut	shut	shut	**teach**	taught	taught
sing	sang	sung	**tear**	tore	torn
sink	sank	sunk	**tell**	told	told
sit	sat	sat	**think**	thought	thought
sleep	slept	slept	**throw**	threw	thrown
slide	slid	slid	**thrust**	thrust	thrust
speak	spoke	spoken	**understand**	understood	understood
speed	sped	sped	**upset**	upset	upset
spend	spent	spent	**wake**	woke	woken
spin	spun	spun	**wear**	wore	worn
split	split	split	**win**	won	won
spread	spread	spread	**withdraw**	withdrew	withdrawn
stand	stood	stood	**write**	wrote	written

TABLE OF CONTENTS

UNIT 1

Subject-Verb Agreement and Tense Consistency

Although the exercises in the grammar units may have thematic topics, you can present the grammar units in whichever order you prefer.

You can use the Preview activity to introduce subject-verb agreement. Students can then complete the unit in class or for homework.

Preview

FIND THE DIFFERENCES

What are six differences between these photos? On a separate sheet of paper, write complete sentences about six differences.

EXAMPLE: In B, there are birds in the sky.

A.

B.

Subject-Verb Agreement: Forms and Usage

PRESENT TENSE AGREEMENT

There are two forms of present tense verbs: the base form and the third-person-singular form. Use the base form when the subject is *I*, *you*, *we*, or *they*.

Lifeguards **take** special courses. I **know** two lifeguards. We **discuss** life-saving techniques.

Add *–s* or *–es* to verbs that follow *he*, *she*, or *it*. In other words, if the subject is one person, place, or thing, but not *you* or *I*, the verb must take an *–s* or *–es* ending.

One person: The doctor **has** many patients.
One place: The clinic **closes** on Sundays.
One thing: The file **contains** personal information.

TIP

Spelling Rules for the Third-Person Singular Form

Add *–es* to verbs ending in *–s*, *–sh*, *–ss*, *–ch*, *–o*, or *–x*.

teach ▶ teach**es** do ▶ do**es**

When a verb ends in a consonant + *–y*, change *–y* to *–ies*.

carry ▶ carr**ies** study ▶ stud**ies**

When a verb ends in a vowel + *–y*, keep the *–y* and add *–s*.

say ▶ say**s** destroy ▶ destroy**s**

PAST TENSE AGREEMENT

Almost all verbs have only one past tense form, so you don't have to modify it when the subject changes. The only verb that requires specific subject-verb agreement in its past tense form is the verb *be*, which has two past forms: *was* and *were*.

I / He / She / It **was** in the living room.
You / We / They **were** in the kitchen.

THERE + BE

When a sentence begins with *There*, the real subject follows the verb *be*.

There **is / was** + one thing: There **was** a fire on Elm Street.
There **are / were** + two or more things: There **were** many firefighters at the site.

SPECIAL SUBJECTS

Gerunds

Sometimes a gerund (*–ing* form of the verb) is the singular subject of a sentence.

Snowboarding requires good reflexes.

Indefinite Pronouns

Indefinite pronouns beginning with *every*, *some*, *any*, or *no* are considered singular. To help remember this rule, notice that the last part of each word is a singular subject.

everybody	everyone	everything	everywhere
somebody	someone	something	somewhere
anybody	anyone	anything	anywhere
nobody	no one	nothing	nowhere

Everyone **has** fears, but nobody **likes** to admit it.

Each* and *Every

If you put one or more singular nouns (joined by *and*) after *each* and *every*, the verb remains singular.

Every firefighter **wears** safety gear. Each man and woman **works** hard.

Agreement with Collective Nouns

Collective nouns refer to groups of people or things. Here are some common collective nouns:

army	class	crowd	group	public
association	club	family	jury	organization
audience	committee	gang	mob	society
band	company	government	population	team

Generally, a group acts as a unit, so you must use it with the singular form of the verb.

The jury **is** ready to read the verdict.

If the members of the group act individually, use the plural form of the verb. It is a good idea to reword the sentence using a phrase such as *members of*.

Acceptable: The jury **are** not able to come to an agreement.
Better: The members of the jury **are** not able to come to an agreement.

Practice

EXERCISE 1 **SUBJECT-VERB AGREEMENT**

Underline and correct ten errors in subject-verb agreement. If you make mistakes, review the rules about special subjects on the previous page.

EXAMPLE: Mark McCrum travel [travels] around the world.

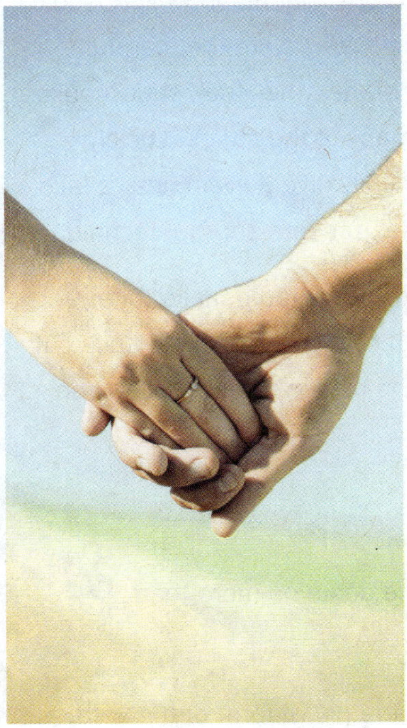

1. Every man and woman share [shares] similar expressions, along with an understanding of their underlying meaning. That's why everybody react [reacts] badly to a frown. But gestures and traditions is [are] not the same all over the world. In his book *Going Dutch in Beijing* Mark McCrum warn [warns] his readers about some cultural faux pas.

2. Many of McCrum's examples is [are] humorous. For example, in Japan, if someone blow [blows] his nose in public, others will be disgusted. Nobody like [likes] to see that. And holding hands are [is] not a sign of romance in many cultures. In Saudi Arabia, for example, a man will grasp another man's hand as a sign of respect. However, when a man and woman holds [hold] hands, it is not culturally acceptable. In South Africa, everyone do [does] a three-part handshake. People should be careful about their gestures when they are abroad.

TIP

Police Is Considered Plural

Many nouns that refer to a group, such as *association*, are collective and are considered singular. *Police* is also a collective noun, but it is thought of as plural because the word *officers* is implied but not stated.

The police **have** a protester in custody.

EXERCISE 2 **AGREEMENT IN PRESENT AND PAST TENSES**

Underline the appropriate verbs in parentheses. Be especially careful with collective nouns.

EXAMPLE: The committee (have / has) five members.

1. Kate is part of a survival club that (have / has) many meetings. Kate's group (meet / meets) once a month. Sometimes, the police (visit / visits) the club to tell the group how to survive in certain scenarios. For example, yesterday, an officer (was / were) a guest. Officer Wells discussed what to do if someone (fall / falls) through the ice. She explained that the body (lose / loses) heat twenty-five times faster in water than in air. Hypothermia (is / are) a likely result of falling through the ice into the lake below.

2. Last year, at our local lake, there (was / were) forty accidents in which people fell through the ice. Many members of the public (was / were) not careful. Some outdoor enthusiasts (was / were) reckless when they took snowmobiles onto the thin ice. Police (was / were) called in many of the cases. Luckily, there (was / were) no fatalities last winter. My family (live / lives) near a lake, and so do many others. These families should learn some survival techniques.

3. At the club, Officer Wells also discussed what to do if a rattlesnake (bite / bites) someone. There (is / are) a common myth that people should suck out the poison. However, (do / does) not suck out the poison! When Wells speaks, the audience always (listen / listens) carefully.

MORE THAN ONE SUBJECT

There are special agreement rules when a sentence contains more than one subject.

And*, *Or*, and *Nor

When two or more subjects are joined by *and*, use the plural form of the verb. However, when subjects are joined by *or* or *nor*, match the verb with the subject closest to it.

➜

Neither Anna **nor** her children **watch** (plural) television.

Either the children **or** Clara **is** (singular) allergic to dust.

As Well As* and *Along With

The interrupting expressions *as well as* and *along with* don't follow the same rules as *and*. They do not form compound subjects. The real subject is before the interrupting expression.

Flora, Jamal, **and** Kaitlin **work** as firefighters.
Flora, **as well as** Jamal and Kaitlin, **works** as a firefighter.

TIP

Two-Verb Constructions

Sometimes two verbs are separated by a noun or pronoun. Examples are "**make** it **work**" or "**help** him **finish**." Look at the following example. Notice that you must use the base form of the second verb.

Milk **makes** Jess **feel** (base form) sick. Sometimes he **helps** me **cook** (base form).

EXERCISE 3 CORRECTING AGREEMENT ERRORS

Underline and correct ten errors in subject-verb agreement.

EXAMPLE: There is [are] some interesting stories of survival against the odds.

1. One survival story makes everyone feels [feel] worried. Do [Does] a GPS device help or harms [harm] drivers? In 2011, Rita Chretien, as well as her husband, Albert, were [was] in Nevada. They had left their home in Penticton, BC, and they were going to Las Vegas. Looking for a shortcut, they was [were] dependent on their GPS. The device led them off-track and into the remote wilderness. According to Chretien, there was [were] no houses in the vicinity.

2. Albert Chretien decided to look for help. For more than forty days, Rita was alone. Neither her husband nor any rescue team were [was] nearby. Candy, as well as some fish-oil pills, were [was] all that Rita had

→

to eat. Finally, on the forty-ninth day, Rita's luck changed. Chad Herman, along with two of his friends, was were looking for antlers. The trio found the very sick Rita, but they never found her husband. Today, Chretien's faith helps her survive survives the loss of her husband.

INTERRUPTING WORDS AND PHRASES

Words that are between the subject and the verb can cause confusion about subject-verb agreement. In such cases, look for the subject and then make sure that the verb agrees with it.

Some books [that I read in my first college course] **are** about nature.

Agreement After Prepositional Phrases

A prepositional phrase is made up of a preposition and its object (a noun or a pronoun). The object of the prepositional phrase is *not* the subject of the sentence. In the following sentence, the subject and verb are "interrupted" by a prepositional phrase.

The man [with the tattoos] **has** red hair.

Be particularly careful with phrases containing *of the*. In the next examples, the subject appears before *of the*.

One **of the** most annoying neighbours in our district **knows** everybody's secrets.
A photo **of the** cars **appears** in the magazine.
Each **of the** photos **is** in colour.

Exception: Expressions of quantity don't follow the preceding *of the* rule. When the subject is an expression of quantity—*the majority of*, *one third of*, *a part of*, *10 percent of*, *the rest of*—the verb agrees with the noun that follows *of* (*the*).

The majority **of the** audience **likes** the show.
About 20 percent **of the** viewers **watch** the program each week.

EXERCISE 4 CORRECTING AGREEMENT ERRORS

In the second sentence in paragraph 1, *majority* refers to "disasters," so the correct answer is *are*. In the second sentence in paragraph 2, *majority* refers to "specialists," so the correct answer is *believe*.

In the following passage, twelve verbs are underlined. Of these, correct the eight verb errors and write *C* over the four correct verbs.

EXAMPLE: About 5 percent of the airline industry's passengers encounter encounters problems during flights.

1. An earthquake, as well as a volcanic eruption or tsunami, is are unpredictable. Although some disasters C claim no lives, the majority are is deadly. After a tragedy, one of the most common reactions is are to panic. According to Dr. Leach, author of *Survivor Psychology*, 95 percent of the population C panics within the first three

hours of living through a disaster. The majority of victims doesn't [don't] know how to react. Only 5 percent of people remains [remain] calm and clear-headed. Even if somebody survive [survives] the physical trauma, he or she may not necessarily survive the psychological trauma.

2. Ultimately, what do specialists know [C] about survival? The majority believes [believe] that good physical and psychological health help [C] people get through a crisis. Maybe everybody have [has] the ability to survive.

INTERRUPTING WORDS: *WHO*, *WHICH*, AND *THAT*

Some sentences include a relative clause beginning with the pronouns *who*, *which*, or *that*. In the relative clause, the verb must agree with the antecedent of *who*, *which*, or *that*.

> She is a writer **who lives** in Jamaica.
> Here are some stories **that explore** unsolved mysteries.
> One book, **which appears** online, **discusses** a secret island.

EXERCISE 5 **AGREEMENT AFTER INTERRUPTING WORDS**

The next adapted excerpt is from the H. G. Wells novel *The Island of Doctor Moreau*. Read the text. Circle the subject of each verb in parentheses and then underline the correct verb form.

EXAMPLE: There is something in the starlight that (loosen / loosens) one's tongue.

1. The cabin in which I (find / finds) myself (is / are) small and rather untidy. A young man who (have / has) flaxen hair, a bristly straw-coloured moustache, and a dropping lip (is / are) sitting and holding my wrist. For a minute, we (stare / stares) at each other without speaking. His watery grey eyes (is / are) oddly void of expression. One of his eyelids (flicker / flickers). Then I hear a sound that (is / are) like the low angry growling of some large animal. The man, who (appear / appears) concerned, (ask / asks), "How do you feel now?"

2. I reply that I (do / does) not recollect how I got here. "You (was / were) picked up in a boat, starving. The name on the boat (is / are) the *Lady Vain*. There (was / were) blood spots on the upper edge of the vessel," he says. "You were in luck," he continues, "to get picked up by a ship that (have / has) a medical man aboard. Those who (was / were) with you did not share the same fate. Each of those creatures (have / has) perished."

AVOID FAULTY TENSE SHIFTS

When you write, don't shift tenses unless the time frame really changes. In the example below, the first sentence is a generalization, while the next three sentences are part of a past tense story.

> I **believe** in bad luck. Last Saturday, I **walked** under a ladder. Suddenly, bad things **began** to happen. First, I **slipped** while I **was carrying** a tray at work. Then I **cut** my finger.

TIP

Would and *Could*

When you tell a story about a past event, use ***would*** instead of *will* and ***could*** instead of *can*.

> In 1850, some doctors ~~will~~ **would** cut patients. People ~~cannot~~ **could not** complain.

EXERCISE 6 **TENSE CONSISTENCY**

Underline and correct six errors involving tense shifts.

EXAMPLE: In 1938, he dieted, but he <u>doesn't</u> (didn't) lose much weight.

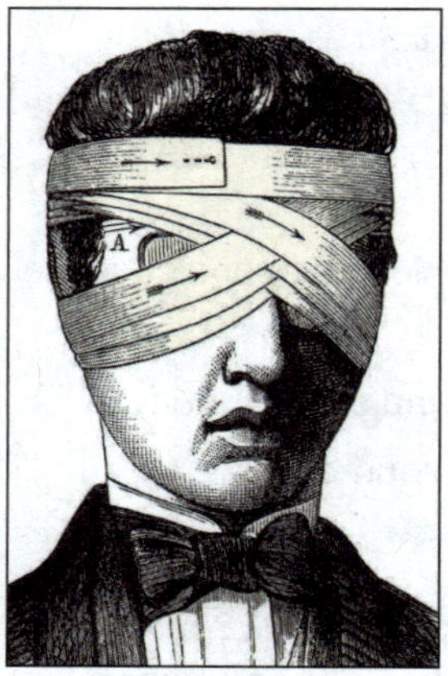

For many centuries, bloodletting and skull drilling were common medical practices. Doctors <u>will</u> (would) cut patients and permit their blood to flow in the false belief that this <u>will</u> (would) balance the patient's system. The practice <u>is</u> (was) common until the nineteenth century. In addition, doctors had an interesting cure for migraines. They <u>can</u> (could) drill small holes directly into a patient's skull. Unsurprisingly, the holes <u>will</u> (would) rarely relieve a patient's headaches. Even these days, many people still <u>chose</u> (choose) unhealthy or suspicious remedies to cure their headaches. Perhaps in the future, some of our modern medical practices will appear ridiculous.

WRITING ABOUT FICTION

When writing about historical events, use the past tense. When writing about a fictional short story or novel, use the present tense to describe the characters and their situations.

> In the 1920s, many great writers **lived** in Paris. A classic Ernest Hemingway novel **describes** the Parisian nightlife. The main characters **meet** in cafés.

EXERCISE 7 WRITING ABOUT FICTION

Underline and correct ten errors involving tense shifts.

1. In 1929, Canadian author Morley Callaghan spends [spent] the summer in Paris. Almost every day, he will [would] join other writers in popular cafés. Callaghan becomes [became] friends with Ernest Hemingway. Their friendship ended after he wins [won] a boxing match against Hemingway.

2. In Paris, Hemingway wrote *The Sun Also Rises*. The novel is about Jake Barns and his relationship with a promiscuous divorcee, Lady Brett Ashley. Ashley cuts her hair short and had [has] modern attitudes. Barns falls in love with her, so her numerous love affairs angered [anger] him. Tensions built [build], and several men had [have] fist fights with each other. Ashley chose [chooses] to return to her former lover, Mike Campbell. In the final scene, Ashley and Barns were [are] in a taxi. They are sad because they won't be together.

UNIT Review

Complete the following exercises. If you don't know an answer, go back and review the appropriate section.

Answers will vary.

1. When should you add –s or –es to verbs? You should add *–s* or *–es* to verbs in the present tense, when the subject is third-person singular.

2. Some indefinite pronouns are singular and require the singular form of a verb. List six singular indefinite pronouns.

anybody	everybody	somebody
anyone	everyone	someone

3. Some nouns are collective and require the singular form of a verb. Underline the five singular collective nouns below.

army	committee	family	police
brothers	crowd	judge	population

4. When should you use *was* or *were*?

   a) Use *was* with verbs in the past tense and subjects *I*, *he*, *she*, and *it*.

   b) Use *were* with verbs in the past tense and subjects *you*, *we*, and *they*.

→

5. Underline and correct the errors in subject-verb agreement in the following sentences.

a) There is [are] many different religions.

b) Either the Edwards sisters or Simon are [is] in the room.

c) One of our cousins live [lives] in Thailand.

d) The majority of the citizens has [have] smartphones.

COMPANION WEB+ Need more practice? Visit the Companion Website and try more grammar exercises.

Final Review

PART A

Underline the appropriate verbs in parentheses.

1. There (is / are) many interesting survival facts. For example, if someone (encounter / encounters) a black bear, one of the worst things to do (is / are) to play dead. Although black bears rarely attack humans, the black bear (welcome / welcomes) easy prey. The majority of the population (believe / believes) that running away is the best option. However, a hungry enough bear often (chase / chases) its prey and can reach speeds of up to 50 kilometres per hour. Speaking gently and backing away slowly (is / are) the best responses. Black bears have poor eyesight. They usually retreat if they hear you speaking and realize you are a human. More than 90 percent of people (don't / doesn't) know those facts.

You can use the Final Review as a test. There are twenty answers in Part A and ten in Part B, for a total of thirty points. You can also find additional practice exercises and testing material on the Companion Website.

2. Another fact that almost nobody (know / knows) concerns riptides. A riptide is a strong current that sometimes (pull / pulls) swimmers out to sea. The majority of swimmers (try / tries) to return to shore. However, such currents are extremely strong, and it is difficult or impossible to swim against them.

3. If you are caught in a riptide, one of the most important things to remember (is / are) to remain calm. In 2009, Romilla Higgens, along with her daughter, (was / were) in shallow water. A tide pulled them out to sea. The police

(was / were) nearby, and one officer ran into the ocean. Either one or several lifeguards (was / were) also nearby. Sadly, neither Higgens nor her daughter (was / were) able to make it to safety.

4. In another case, Stephanie Hayes was swimming with her sons when a riptide began to pull them out. Luckily, each of them (was / were) aware of safety procedures. They (was / were) calm as the current pulled them away from the beach, and then they swam out of the current, to the side, instead of toward the shore. After the incident, Hayes, as well as her two sons, (was / were) safe. Everybody (need / needs) to learn about riptide safety procedures.

PART B

Underline and correct ten errors in subject-verb agreement and/or tense shifts.

5. Annually, there is [are] more than ten thousand car-submersion accidents in North America. Apparently, during car submersions, many people panic and forgets [forget] to remove their seat belts. In addition, the majority of people tries [try] to open the car door, but once the lower part of the door is underwater, the door was [is] almost impossible to open. Finally, one of the biggest mistakes are [is] when trapped drivers or passengers in cars with electric windows wait too long to open the windows. After these cars hit the water, the electric motors that operates [operate] the windows can stop working.

6. For example, in 2006, Archie Allen accidentally drove his car into the Chester River in Maryland. After the car hit the water, Allen's electric window won't [wouldn't] open. He thought that he will [would] die. Luckily, he can [could] escape from a rear window and he swims [swam] to shore. He was lucky to survive.

SPEAKING AND WRITING

Students can do the writing exercise on a separate sheet of paper. Once students have finished, ask them to exchange their writing and peer edit for subject-verb agreement and tense consistency.

An Admirable Person

Work with a partner. First, describe someone whom you admire. What are the person's best qualities? Give specific examples of that person's actions that are admirable. Then, listen as your partner does the same for someone he or she admires. When you finish, write a paragraph about your partner and the person that he or she has chosen.

UNIT 2

Present, Past, and Future Tenses

You can use the Preview activity to review present, past, and future tenses. Students can also review question forms.

In a computer lab, give students five minutes to read about one of the events. Then, in teams, they can report back on what happened and construct their questions.

Preview

MEMORABLE EVENTS

Work with a partner. Choose one of the following photos of a memorable event, or choose a more recent event. On a piece of paper, do the following:

- Write five sentences to explain what happened.
- Then write six questions about the event. Write two questions concerning the past, two questions concerning the present, and two questions concerning the future.

A.

Japan
Tsunami and nuclear meltdown
March 11, 2011

B.

Quebec
Student strike
Spring 2012

Verb Tenses: Forms and Usage

PRESENT TENSES

Compare the **simple present** and the **present progressive** tenses.

Jeremy **works** every Saturday as a lifeguard. (simple present)

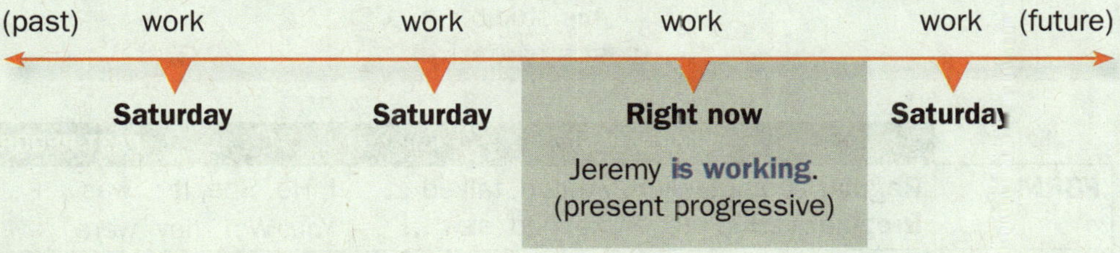

	SIMPLE PRESENT (GENERAL)	PRESENT PROGRESSIVE (NOW OR TEMPORARY PERIOD)
FORM	I, You, We, They } like. He, She, It } likes.	I am + verb + –ing. He, She, It is + verb + –ing. You, We, They are + verb + –ing.
USAGE	Indicates general truths, facts, habitual actions, and customs. Some nations **have** oil. (fact) Alicia **travels** every winter. (habit) Devout Muslims **fast** during Ramadan. (custom) **Keywords:** always, often, usually, sometimes, seldom, rarely, never, every day ...	Indicates that an action is happening now or for a present, temporary period of time. Right now, we **are eating** lunch. (now) This week, Jamil **is taking** a break. (temporary period of time) **Keywords:** now, at this moment, currently, today, these days, this week, this month, this morning ...
QUESTION	Put *do* or *does* before the subject. Use the base form of the verb. **Do** you often travel? **Does** she have a passport? **Exception:** *be* **Is** the plane late? **Are** they happy?	Put *be* before the subject. **Am** I bothering you? **Is** she sleeping now? **Are** they staying with us?
NEGATIVE	Add *do* or *does* + *not*. The train **does not** provide food. (doesn't) They **do not** own a car. (don't) **Exception:** *be* They are **not** late. (aren't)	Add *not*. He is **not** sleeping right now. (isn't) They are **not** working today. (aren't)

PAST TENSES

Compare the **simple past** and the **past progressive** tenses.

Yesterday, Khaleb **was cleaning** his studio when the fire **started**.

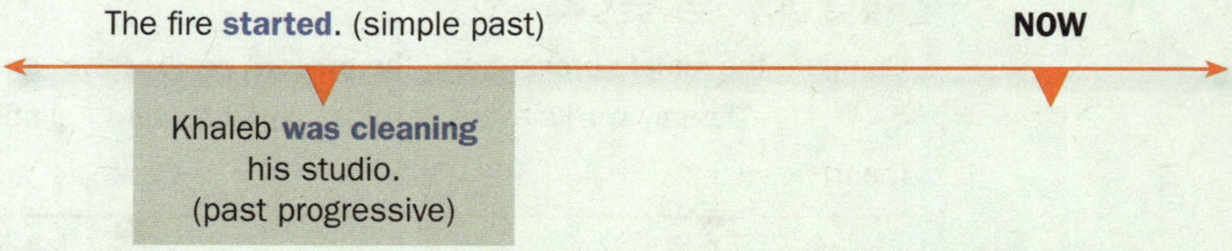

	SIMPLE PAST	PAST PROGRESSIVE
FORM	**Regular verbs:** looked, wanted, talked … **Irregular verbs:** ate, broke, had, saw …	I, He, She, It was + verb + *–ing*. You, We, They were + verb + *–ing*.
USAGE	The **simple past** indicates that an action was completed at a definite time in the past. Last week, we **bought** plane tickets. **Keywords:** ago, yesterday, last week, when I was a child, many years ago, once upon a time …	The **past progressive** shows that an action was in progress at a specific past time. It can also show that a past action was interrupted. Yesterday at 1 a.m., we **were sleeping**. (specific past time) While I **was eating** lunch, the phone rang. (interrupted action) **Keywords:** as, when, while, during, at 4 a.m., at noon …
QUESTION	Put *did* before the subject. Use the base form of the verb. **Did** you **travel** last year? **Did** they **help** you? **Exception:** *be* **Was** Julie late? **Were** you angry?	Put *be* before the subject. **Was** he **speaking** loudly at 1 a.m.? **Were** they **waiting** for me at noon?
NEGATIVE	Add *did* + *not*. Julie **did not** complain yesterday. (didn't) They **did not** travel last year. (didn't) **Exception:** *be* They were **not** late. (weren't)	Add *not*. He was **not** speaking loudly at 1 a.m. (wasn't) They were **not** waiting for me at noon. (weren't)

FUTURE TENSES

FORM	USAGE	EXAMPLE
will + verb	• prediction • spontaneous action or gesture of willingness	It **will rain** soon. I**'ll pay** for the meal. She**'ll do** it!
be going to + verb	• prediction • previously planned action	It **is going to rain** soon. I**'m going to leave**.

SPELLING OF VERB FORMS ENDING IN *–ING* OR *–ED*

BASE FORM	*–ING* ENDING	*–ED* ENDING	SPELLING RULES
smoke	smoking	smoked	***–ing*:** When verbs end in *–e*, drop the *–e* and add *–ing*. ***–ed*:** When verbs end in *–e*, simply add *–d*.
One-Syllable Verbs			
stop	stopping	stopped	When one-syllable verbs end in a consonant-vowel-consonant, double the last letter and add *–ing* or *–ed*. **Exceptions:** Never double the last letter of verbs ending in *–x* or *–w* (*snowing*, *fixing*). Also, double the last letter of *quit* (*quitting*) and *quiz* (*quizzed*) even though they have two vowels; the *qu* sounds like the consonants *kw*.
Multi-Syllable Verbs			
visit develop	visiting developing	visited developed	When the final syllable is not stressed in verbs ending in a consonant-vowel-consonant, add *–ing* or *–ed*.
refer omit	referring omitting	referred omitted	When the final syllable is stressed in verbs ending in a consonant-vowel-consonant, double the last letter and add *–ing* or *–ed*.
Verbs Ending in *–y* or *–ie*			
enjoy	enjoying	enjoyed	When verbs end in a vowel + *–y*, just add *–ing* or *–ed*.
worry carry	worrying carrying	worried carried	When verbs end in a consonant + *–y*, just add *–ing*. However, when forming the past tense, change *–y* to *–i* and add *–ed*.
tie	tying	tied	When verbs end in *–ie*, change the *–ie* to *–y* and add *–ing*. When forming the past tense, just add *–d*.

Pronounce the next words out loud and ask students to spell the past or progressive forms: *open, begin, visit, omit, enter, prefer, deliver, happen, occur,* and *decipher*.

PRONUNCIATION HELP WITH ONLINE DICTIONARIES

Many dictionaries are available online. On some sites, such as *dictionary.reference.com*, a word's stressed syllable is indicated in bold, and by clicking on the loudspeaker icon, you can hear the pronunciation of the word.

be • gin • ning [bih-**gin**-ing]

Practice

EXERCISE 1 **PRESENT TENSES**

Underline the correct verb forms in the parentheses below. Then identify the usage of each of these verbs. Write *G* if the verb refers to a general fact or habit. Write *N* if it refers to an action that is happening now or for a temporary period of time.

EXAMPLE: What (is she reading / does she read) __N__ right now?

1. Frequently, Brigitte Fortin (is having / have / has) __G__ flashbacks to a serious car accident she was involved in. In fact, right now, she (is talking / talk / talks) __N__ about it with her husband. Brigitte (is wanting / want / wants) __G__ to forget about the crash, but she (isn't knowing / doesn't know / →

don't knows) __G__ how to do it. At this moment, she (is crying / cry / cries) __N__ because she remembers how terrified she was when her brakes stopped working. Her car left the road and flipped over three times. She spent three months in the hospital. This month she (take / takes / is taking) __N__ anxiety medication.

2. People rarely (are retaining / retain / retains) __G__ strong memories about physical pain. If they did, women would never have more than one baby. Emotional pain and fear, however, (are lasting / last / lasts) __G__ for a long time in people's minds. Today, Alex Fortin (is driving / drive / drives) __N__ on a highway for the first time since his wife's accident. Right now, his wife (is talking / talk / talks) __N__ to him from the passenger seat. Alex always (is driving / drive / drives) __G__ carefully.

EXERCISE 2 REGULAR AND IRREGULAR PAST TENSE VERBS

Write the past tense form of the following regular and irregular verbs. (See Appendix 1 on page 149 for a list of common irregular past tense verbs.)

EXAMPLES: watch ___watched___ say ___said___

Regular		Irregular	
1. spy	spied	**8.** ring	rang
2. stay	stayed	**9.** bring	brought
3. rely	relied	**10.** lead	led
4. employ	employed	**11.** think	thought
5. snap	snapped	**12.** drink	drank
6. prefer	preferred	**13.** choose	chose
7. mention	mentioned	**14.** keep	kept

COMPANION WEB+ Visit the Companion Website for more practice spelling past tense verbs.

SIMPLE PAST AND PAST PROGRESSIVE

Use the past progressive to describe a past action that was in progress. Do not overuse the past progressive tense. Never use it to talk about past habits or a series of past actions.

Past habit: Joshua ~~was playing~~ **played** guitar when he was younger.

Series of past actions: Last night, he ~~was singing~~ **sang**, ~~was dancing~~ **danced**, and ~~was playing~~ **played** the drums.

EXERCISE 3 PRESENT AND PAST TENSES

Fill in the blanks with the correct form of the verbs in parentheses. Use present and past tenses, as appropriate.

EXAMPLE: In 1977, the Beverly Hills Supper Club fire (kill) killed over 150 people.

1. Nowadays, almost nobody (remember) remembers the Station nightclub fire that (occur) occurred in Rhode Island on February 20, 2003. The fire (be) was one of the deadliest nightclub fires in America. One hundred people (lose) lost their lives in the blaze.

2. That night, just after 11:00 p.m., Great White, a popular rock band, (step) stepped onto the stage. The fire (start) started while the band (play) was playing "Desert Moon." The soundproofing foam behind the drummer (begin) began to burn. Initially, audience members (be) were calm as the flame flickered. Maybe they (think) thought that the flames were part of the show.

3. A journalist who (film) was filming the show captured people's reactions. At first, most people (move, not) didn't move. They (stand) stood still while one man (point) was pointing frantically at the exit. Two minutes later, while the room (fill) was filling with smoke, everyone panicked and (run) ran toward the front door.

4. Often during fires, people (remember, not) don't remember that buildings have several fire exits. Most people (go) go toward the main entrance. On that night in 2003, the crowd (block) blocked / was blocking the front door, so people couldn't leave. Very few people (leave) left by the other four exits. During a fire, it (be) is important to react quickly. Even if one door is blocked, there (be) are usually other ways to leave a building.

NON-PROGRESSIVE VERBS

The verbs below are not generally used in the progressive tense because they indicate an ongoing state rather than a temporary action.

PREFERENCE		STATE		POSSESSION	PERCEPTION	
admire	like	agree	realize	belong	appear*	seem
appreciate	love	believe	recognize	have*	hear	smell*
care	mind	consist	refuse	own	imagine	sound*
desire	need	cost	remember	possess	notice	taste*
despise	prefer	doubt	think*		see	weigh*
envy	want	forget	trust			
hate		know	understand			
		mean				

* Some verbs have more than one meaning and can be used in the progressive tense. Compare the following pairs of sentences.

Progressive	Non-Progressive
He **is having** a bad day.	He **has** two Picassos. (expresses possession)
I **am thinking** about money.	I **think** it is expensive. (expresses an opinion)
She **is weighing** herself.	She **weighs** 130 pounds. (expresses a fact)

EXERCISE 4 IDENTIFY ERRORS IN SIMPLE AND PROGRESSIVE VERBS

In the following sentences, underline and correct present or past tense errors. Write *C* beside sentences that are correct.

was resting
EXAMPLE: That morning, everyone rest when the engine started to burn.

survive
1. Occasionally, people are surviving plane crashes.

crashed
2. In May of 2010, a plane was crashing in Libya.

did the plane crash
3. Why the plane crashed?

was
4. The plane be flying over a desert when the engine failed.

were there
5. Why there were so many casualties?

6. Only one child ~~did~~ survived.

7. Amazingly, the ten-year old child had only a few leg fractures. C

determined
8. In October 2010, Libyan authorities were determining the cause of the crash.

were
9. They claimed that poor landing equipment and pilot error was the main causes of the crash.

do not believe
10. A lot of people are not believing that flying is safe.

think
11. They are thinking that airplanes are dangerous.

12. Flying in an airplane is safer than driving on a highway. C

SUBJECT AND OBJECT QUESTIONS

When using *who*, *what*, *how much*, or *how many* to ask about the **subject** of a question, you don't need an auxiliary.

Lena lives with Jonas.	**The car** hit a fence.	**Fifty** paintings survived.
↑	↑	↑
Who lives with Jonas?	**What** hit a fence?	**How many** paintings survived?

When using *who(m)*,* *what*, *how much*, or *how many* to ask about the **object** of a question, you must add an auxiliary to the question.

Lena lived with **Jonas**.	The car hit **a fence**.	She had **fifty** paintings.
Who(m) did Lena live with?	**What did** the car hit?	**How many** paintings **did** she have?

* *Whom* is used in formal and academic English. In informal English, it is acceptable to use *who*.

EXERCISE 5 QUESTIONS

Change the following sentences into questions. Answers to the questions are in bold.

EXAMPLE: **A tsunami** hit Thailand.
What hit Thailand?

1. Tilly Smith lives **in England**.
   Where does Tilly Smith (she) live?
2. She is thinking about **the past** right now.
   What is she thinking about right now?
3. She learned about tsunamis **in 2004**.
   When did she learn about tsunamis?
4. She went **to Phuket**.
   Where did she go?
5. Her family stayed in a hotel **for three weeks**.
   How long did her family stay in a hotel?
6. She knew **a tsunami was coming**.
   What did she know?
7. She warned **her parents** about the tsunami.
   Who(m) did she warn about the tsunami?
8. **Tilly** saved many people.
   Who saved many people?
9. She asked **a guard** to evacuate the beach.
   Who(m) did she ask to evacuate the beach?

→

10. She wanted people to leave the beach **because she recognized the warning signs of a coming tsunami**.

Why did she want people to leave the beach?

11. People **were running** when the giant waves arrived.

What were people doing when the giant waves arrived?

12. **The hotel lobby** became full of rushing water.

What became full of rushing water?

13. **Hundreds** of people survived.

How many people survived?

14. She will return to Thailand **next summer**.

When will she return to Thailand?

15. She is going to stay **at the same hotel**.

Where is she going to stay?

FUTURE TENSES

Use *will* or *be going to* when you predict the future. For previously planned actions, use *be going to*. For spontaneous actions, use *will*.

Prediction:	The population **will grow**. It **is going to explode**.
Planned:	I found a job. I **am going to work** in London.
Spontaneous:	The doorbell is ringing. I **will answer** it.

TIP

Present Tenses

Sometimes the present tenses can refer to a future time. The **present progressive** can refer to a previously planned event that will happen soon. The **simple present** can refer to schedules and timetables.

We **are leaving** tonight. The show **starts** in two hours.

Answers will vary.

EXERCISE 6 FUTURE TENSES

Fill in the blanks with the appropriate future tense form of the verbs in parentheses. Note that in some instances, there is more than one possible answer.

EXAMPLE: If you are having problems, I (help) will help you.

1. Noah: In the election, who (you, vote) are you going to vote / are you voting for?

2. Anna: I'm not sure. Maybe I (support) will support the left-leaning candidate. On the other hand, she (raise) is going to raise taxes. At least, she said she would in her campaign literature.

3. Noah: Perhaps she has to. How (we, pay) ___are we going to pay / will we pay___ for rising health care costs?

4. Anna: Please don't try to influence me. Maybe I just (vote, not) ___won't vote___. My vote probably (make, not) ___won't make___ a difference, anyway.

5. Noah: Don't think that way. Listen, I (watch) ___am going to watch / am watching___ the debate tonight. Why don't you watch it with me?

6. Anna: I can't. My train (leave) ___is leaving / leaves / is going to leave___ at 8 p.m.

7. Noah: Your train left ten minutes ago! Wait here while I get my keys. I (drive) ___will drive___ you home.

TIME CLAUSES IN FUTURE TENSE SENTENCES

A time clause begins with a **time marker** such as those below. When describing the future, use the present tense after the time marker.

after	as soon as	before	unless	until
as long as	in case	when	whatever	whenever

The time marker can appear in the first or second part of the sentence.

After I **finish** college, I **will travel**.
Caleb **will call** us as soon as he **arrives**.

TIP

Never Write *Gonna*

Although people say *gonna*, it isn't a proper word. Always write *going to*.

I'm ~~gonna~~ **going to** finish this project.

EXERCISE 7 FUTURE TENSES AND TIME CLAUSES

PART A

Circle the time markers in the sentences below. Then underline and correct all verb errors.

EXAMPLE: I will leave (as soon as) I will finish [finish] my work.

1. (When) the spring will arrive [arrives], will there be any floods?

2. Tomorrow, the roads will be slippery (after) the freezing rain will come [comes].

→

3. **(As soon as)** the sea levels will rise [rise], there will be a lot of flooding.

4. Other problems will occur **(unless)** nations will reduce [reduce] their greenhouse gases.

5. **(After)** the election is over and some time will pass [passes], will the situation change?

PART B

Underline and correct five errors involving future tenses.

6. Scientists predict that major earthquakes will occur on the Pacific coast of North America. What are citizens gonna [going to] do? How big ^[is] the next earthquake going to be? When such disasters will occur [occur], will the coastline change? Where residents are [are residents] going to live after a catastrophe? Unless engineers and construction companies will work [work] together to build more earthquake-proof structures, many buildings and bridges will probably collapse.

AVOIDING DOUBLE NEGATIVES

Double negatives contain two negative words that cancel each other out. To correct double negatives, either remove one of the two negative forms, or change *no* to *any*.

Double Negative	Possible Corrections
She **doesn't** have **no** children.	She doesn't have children. (Remove *no*.) She has no children. (Remove *doesn't*.) She doesn't have any children. (Change *no* to *any*.)

EXERCISE 8 **IDENTIFY ERRORS** Answers will vary.

Underline and correct the errors in the sentences below. Write *C* beside the sentences that are correct.

EXAMPLE: Yesterday, in class, did you heard [hear] about the dog who survived on a deserted island?

1. A few years ago, Jan Griffth decided to took [take] a boat ride with her dog Sophie.

2. When Sophie fell overboard, Jan didn't have no [didn't have any / had no] idea if the dog was dead or alive.

3. What did happen [happened] to the dog?

survive
4. The dog swam across six miles of shark-infested water to survived.

5. Sophie swam all the way to a tiny island. C

didn't think anybody / thought nobody
6. Jan didn't think nobody was going to find her dog.

found
7. Amazingly, while rangers were walking on the beach, they were finding the dog.

agree
8. Most people are agreeing that it is extremely rare for a dog to survive in shark-infested waters.

takes
9. Jan will probably panic if she will take another boat ride.

anymore
10. Today, Jan doesn't own Sophie no more because the dog passed away a few years ago.

UNIT Review

Complete the following exercises. If you don't know an answer, go back and review the appropriate section.

1. Underline and correct the errors in the sentences below. Then explain why the sentences were incorrect.

   EXAMPLE: Every day, he is complaining about something. complains
   Rule: Don't use the present progressive with habitual actions.

   a) Last year, I was working every weekend. worked
   Rule: Don't use the past progressive with habitual past actions.

   b) Last year, did you studied a second language? study
   Rule: In past tense questions, use the base form of the main verb.

   c) Vince wanted to talked with you. talk
   Rule: Use the base form of the verb after *to*.

   d) He will arrive when he will finish work. finishes
   Rule: Do not use future tenses in time clauses.

   e) We don't need no education. don't need any / need no
   Rule: Do not use *not* along with another negative word such as *no*.

2. Write the simple past forms of the following verbs.

   EXAMPLE: bring brought

   a) fall fell
   b) sing sang
   c) teach taught
   d) think thought

Need more practice? Visit the Companion Website and try more exercises about verb tenses.

Final Review

You can use the Final Review as a test. There are fifteen answers in Part A and five answers each in Part B and C, for a total of twenty-five points. You can also find additional practice exercises and testing material on the Companion Website.

PART A

Write the correct form of each verb in parentheses. Use past, present, or future tenses.

EXAMPLE: Some plane crashes (be, not) aren't necessarily fatal.

1. My mother (like, not) doesn't like to be in an airplane. Why (they, refuse) do they refuse to fly? When you (save) save enough money, will you fly in an airplane?

2. Although flying is safer than driving, accidents can occur. In 1960, the members of the Minneapolis Lakers NBA squad (have) had a dangerous journey on a Butler Aviation aircraft. During a period of turbulence, while the athletes (play) were playing cards, the lights inside the plane suddenly (go) went out. The plane (become) became very cold.

3. What (the pilots, do) did the pilots do? They (be) were calm. There was a lot of ice and frost on the windshield, and the plane (have, not) didn't have a defroster. The pilots couldn't see the ground easily. They (know) knew that they would have to land as soon as possible. With each passing minute, the plane (run) was running out of fuel. Their navigational systems were down, so, using physical clues instead, they (find) found a safe place to land.

4. The NBA team members (be, not) weren't sure if they would survive. Fifteen minutes later, the plane crashed in an Iowa cornfield. Amazingly, the crew and passengers (die, not) didn't die.

PART B

Underline and correct five errors involving verb tenses or double negatives.

take
EXAMPLE: The men didn't took precautions.

5. The players ~~didn't know nothing~~ *didn't know / knew nothing / didn't know anything* about the plane's true situation. The pilots ~~were wanting~~ *wanted* to find an adequate place to land the plane. The passengers ~~was~~ *were* really lucky that they were alive: about 60 metres in front of the plane, there was a deep gorge! Today, Butler Aviation doesn't exist ~~no more~~ *anymore*. In the future, when I ~~will fly~~ *fly*, I will appreciate the pilots.

PART C

Change the following sentences into questions. Answers to the questions are in bold.

EXAMPLE: He is talking about **the Lakers**.
Who is he talking about?

6. The pilot wanted to postpone the flight **because of poor weather conditions**.
Why did the pilot want to postpone the flight?

7. The pilot was **resting** when the lights went out.
What was the pilot doing when the lights went out?

8. The movie will be about **the accident**.
What will the movie be about?

9. He flies **every month**.
How often (or When) does he fly?

10. They are discussing **the movie** right now.
What are they discussing right now?

SPEAKING AND WRITING

Students can do the writing exercise on a separate sheet of paper. Once they have finished, ask them to exchange their writing and peer edit for correct use of present, past, and future verb tenses.

Vivid Verbs

With a partner, brainstorm to come up with ten verbs that describe very specific actions. Examples of specific verbs are *whimper*, *sniffle*, *slurp*, and *wrestle*. Refer to your *Avenues 3: English Skills* book or use your dictionary to find good examples of verbs. Write your complete list on a sheet of paper. Then exchange sheets with another team. You and your partner must then write a paragraph incorporating the other team's list of ten verbs. Use the present, past, and future tenses in your paragraph.

UNIT 3 Present Perfect Tenses

Use the Preview activity to introduce students to present perfect tenses.

Preview

LIE DETECTOR

Write three sentences about yourself. Two of the sentences should describe true things that you have done in your life. One of your sentences should describe a lie. Later, you will pretend that you have also done that action. Do not indicate which sentence is a lie. For example, consider the following sentences:

I have danced on a street.	(true)
I have travelled to Brazil.	(false)
I have taken singing classes.	(true)

Show the sentences to a small team of fellow students. You must pretend that all of the sentences are true. Then, your classmates will ask you questions to discover which sentence is a lie. Invent answers for the false story. The team will then have to guess which sentence is true.

Statement 1: ____________________

Statement 2: ____________________

Statement 3: ____________________

Present Perfect: Forms and Usage

Combine a past participle with *have* or *has* to form the present perfect tense. You can use this tense in two different circumstances:

1. To indicate that an action began in the past and continues to the present time.

2008
Leo began his job.

Now
Leo still works here.

Leo **has worked** here since 2008.
(The event began in 2008 and continues to the present time.)

Keywords: never, ever, not yet, so far, up to now, since, for ...

2. To indicate that one or more completed past actions occurred at unspecified past times.

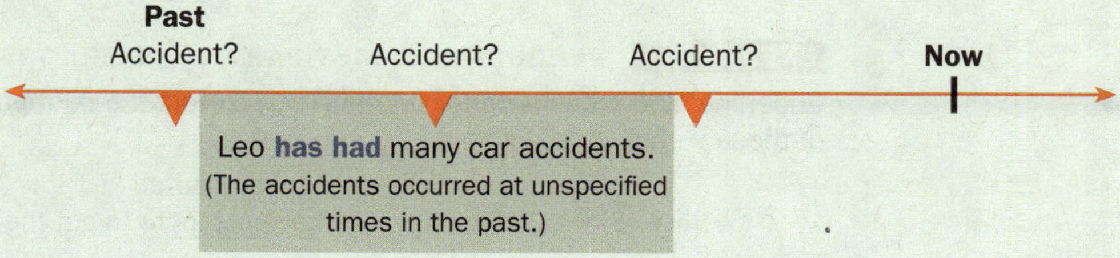

PRESENT PERFECT FORMS

FORM	I / You / We / They } **have** + past participle (eaten, seen, etc.)	He / She / It } **has** + past participle (gone, broken, etc.)
QUESTION	Move the auxiliary (*have* or *has*) before the subject. **Have** you ever **met** Donald?	**Has** Joe **been** to China?
NEGATIVE	Put *not* after *have* or *has*. I **have not met** Donald. (haven't)	Joe **has not been** to China. (hasn't)

SINCE, *FOR*, AND *AGO*

Since refers to a specific past moment when the action began.
For refers to the amount of time that the action has lasted.
Ago refers to a time in the past when the completed action occurred. Use *ago* with the past tense only.

Luis **has lived** in Calgary **since** 2008. (He is still living there.)

He **has worked** as a dentist **for** three years. (He still works as a dentist.)

He **married** Kara six years **ago**.

PRESENT PERFECT PROGRESSIVE TENSE

The present perfect progressive indicates that an action has been in progress from a past time up to the present moment. It emphasizes the *duration* of the uninterrupted activity.

Form: *have/has been* + base form of verb + *–ing*

Rajiv **has been singing** for twenty minutes. When will he stop singing?

With some verbs (e.g., *live*, *work*, *teach*, *study*), the present perfect and the present perfect progressive forms have essentially the same meaning. Compare the following sentences:

Rajiv **has been working** full-time since 2010. }
Rajiv **has worked** full-time since 2010. } Same meaning

Practice

EXERCISE 1 **RECOGNIZING PAST PARTICIPLE ERRORS**

Underline nine present perfect verbs. Then correct the past participle errors in six of those verbs.

competed

EXAMPLE: Since 2010, two cities <u>have compete</u> to get the government contract.

thought

1. Many Canadians <u>have thinked</u> about their cultural identity. They <u>have questioned</u> what it means to be Canadian.

fought

Sometimes, people in one region <u>have fight</u> against those in another. For example, there <u>have been</u> rivalries between Toronto and Montreal or between Edmonton and Calgary. In 2007, Canadian filmmaker Albert Nerenberg produced

heard

a film called *Let's All Hate Toronto*. <u>Have</u> you ever <u>heared</u> of that film?

won

2. What do people around the globe think about Canadians? Our hockey players <u>have win</u> respect. Canada <u>has produced</u> fine actors and comedians. Directors

made

such as David Cronenberg <u>have maked</u> internationally recognized films.

gained

Canadians <u>have</u> also <u>gain</u> a reputation for being nice and self-effacing. Author Douglas Coupland once said, "Canadians can easily pass for Americans as long as we don't accidentally use metric measurements or apologize when hit by a car."

USING AN AUXILIARY WITH *HAVE*

In the present perfect tense, even when the main verb is *have*, you must still use the auxiliary *have* or *has*. Then use the past participle form of the main verb, *had*.

Matt **has had** several car accidents.
We **have had** many discussions about his driving.

EXERCISE 2 **SIMPLE PAST AND PRESENT PERFECT**

Fill in the blanks using the verbs and tenses indicated.

PART A SIMPLE PAST: THE ACTION WAS OVER AT A KNOWN PAST TIME.

EXAMPLE: David and William Horsley (film) Hollywood's first movie. filmed

1. Before the movie industry arrived, Hollywood (be) a quiet suburb. was
2. Filmmakers (avoid) strict patent laws by relocating to Hollywood. avoided
3. The Nestor company (open) the first movie studio in Hollywood. opened
4. In the 1930s, there (be) five major studios in Hollywood. were

PART B PRESENT PERFECT: THE ACTION BEGAN IN THE PAST AND CONTINUES TO THE PRESENT.

EXAMPLE: Over ninety years (pass) since the film industry began. have passed

5. Since the 1920s, studios (try) to create hit films. have tried
6. People (have) dreams about fame ever since. have had
7. The Hollywood Walk of Fame (exist) since 1927. has existed
8. For almost one hundred years, tourists (visit) Hollywood. have visited

PART C PRESENT PERFECT: ONE OR MORE ACTIONS OCCURRED AT UNKNOWN PAST TIMES.

EXAMPLE: I (see) many great films. have seen

9. Millions of people (walk) on Sunset Boulevard. have walked
10. Over the years, many films (have) stereotypical villains. have had
11. Ryan Reynolds (be) in many popular films. has been
12. Canada (produce) a lot of great film directors. has produced

LOOKING AT KEYWORDS

Use keywords to help you decide what tense to use. Be careful: when the past time is stated and other sentences give details about that past time, use the past tense.

Padma Kumar **has been** a set designer **since** she graduated from college. Four years **ago**, she **moved** to England. She **stayed** in a small youth hostel in London, and she **went** to several plays.

TIP

Since and *For*

Point out that sentences with the word *ago* require past tense verbs, because *ago* indicates that the actions were finished at a known past time.

Since refers to a specific past moment when the action began. ***For*** refers to the amount of time that the action has lasted.

He has lived here **since** May. I've known him **for** three months.

EXERCISE 3 **SIMPLE PAST OR PRESENT PERFECT**

PART A

Complete the following sentences using either the past or the present perfect tense of the verb. In each case, underline the keywords or phrases that indicate which tense should be used.

EXAMPLE: We (see) have seen a lot of movies this year.

1. Over the years, Hollywood films (present) have presented many stereotypes. From the 1920s to the 1970s, Caucasian actors often (portray) portrayed Africans and Asians. Cowboy movies were often the worst. During the mid-20th century, Caucasians in redface makeup (pretend) pretended to be Native Americans.

2. Over sixty years ago, Truman Capote (write) wrote the well-received book *Breakfast at Tiffany's* about a country girl who moves to Manhattan. In the story, a photographer, Mr. Yunioshi, lives upstairs from her. In 1961, Hollywood (release) released a movie that was based on the novel. At that time, most people (think) thought that the movie was excellent. But ever since its debut, the film (receive, also) has also received criticism. In the film, a small white actor plays the role of Mr. Yunioshi. The actor wears yellowface makeup and large fake teeth. Ever since 1961, the movie (be) has been a prime example of stereotyping in Hollywood films.

3. Since the mid-1970s, studios (make) have made fewer mistakes of this sort. But some films still rely on stereotypes. For instance, in the 1990s, lawyers (be) were often the bad guys in movies. And for the last few years, many films (have) have had Middle Eastern villains.

PART B

Complete the definitions and examples below using *since*, *for*, or *ago*.

4. ___Ago___ refers to a past time when the action was completed. For example, "The movie hit theatres three months ___ago___."

5. ___Since___ refers to a specific past moment when the action began. The action continues to the present time. For example, "Luc has been a professional actor ___since___ 2010."

6. ___For___ refers to a period of time. For example, "We've been waiting in line ___for___ three hours."

COMPANION web+ For more practice using *since*, *for*, and *ago*, visit the Companion Website.

REVIEW THE SIMPLE PAST AND PRESENT PERFECT FORMS

Look at the differences between the past and present perfect tenses.

Present Perfect
Times are unknown.
Keywords: once, twice, many times …
? ? ?

Specific Past Time **Now**

Present Perfect
Past action continues to the present time.
Keywords: since, for …

Simple Past
Past time is known.
Keywords: ago, last week, yesterday …

Simple past: In 2003, Rihanna **left** Barbados for the first time.
(The event occurred at a known past time.)

Present perfect: She **has sung** since she was three years old.
(The action began in the past and continues to the present.)

She **has returned** to Barbados many times.
(We do not know each date that she visited the country.)

EXERCISE 4 IDENTIFYING REASONS FOR TENSE USAGE

Fill in the blanks with either the present perfect or simple past tense of the verbs. Then explain your choices.

EXAMPLE: Paul (live) with me since March. ___has lived___

Reason: The action began in the past (March) and continues to the present.

1. Paul (go) to Cyprus last May. ___went___

Reason: ___The action finished at a known past time.___

→

2. In Cyprus, Turks and Greeks (fight) for hundreds of years. have fought / have been fighting

Reason: The action began in the past and continues to the present.

3. Paul (visit) many countries since 2005. has visited

Reason: The action was repeated at unknown past times.

4. He (move) to Kingston three years ago. moved

Reason: The action finished at a known past time.

5. Paul and Keira (live) in Kingston since then. have lived

Reason: The action began in the past and continues to the present.

PAST TENSE REMINDER

Use the past tense when referring to someone who is no longer living or to an event that occurred at a known past time. Use the present perfect tense only when the action refers to someone or something that still exists.

Early humans ~~have carved~~ **carved** arrows out of stone.
Weapons **have evolved** over the years.

EXERCISE 5 SIMPLE PAST OR PRESENT PERFECT

Fill in the blanks with the simple past or present perfect form of the verbs.

EXAMPLE: Dr. Aboud (study) has studied many different children.

1. Thousands of years ago, ancient humans (feel) felt suspicious of people from other tribes. They (build) built stone weapons that they (use) used to attack each other. But since the first humans walked on Earth, people (also, develop) have also developed the ability to cooperate and to overlook differences. Can people overcome racial prejudice? Over the years, many psychologists and sociologists (study) have studied this issue.

2. According to psychology professor Frances Aboud, "Discrimination is wired into the brain at conception." Since 1975, she (specialize) has specialized in research on childhood racial awareness. She (perform) has performed many different studies. Over the years, she (test) has tested thousands of children. During the 1980s, she (run)

ran a simple test: she (show) showed children pairs of drawings of either boys or girls that were identical except for skin tone. Then she asked questions such as "Who is mean?" or "Who is nice?" During her tests, about 60 percent of five-year-olds (attribute) attributed negative traits to people of colours different from their own. Aboud says that eight is "the age of reason," when children discover that there are other perspectives and that people of all colours can be both positive and negative.

3. Aboud states that tolerance can be learned more through actions than through words. For instance, Aboud (travel) has travelled to over thirty different nations, and she (interview) has interviewed thousands of people. She says, "When someone (have) has had many experiences working intimately with those of other races, that person stops caring about skin tone." In 1988, Aboud (publish) published her first book, *Children and Prejudice*. Since then, she (write) has written several other books about her research.

QUESTION WORDS

Have you ever ...?

Use this form to determine if something happened at an indefinite past time. Use *never* to specify that something hasn't occurred in a person's life.

Have you ever been to Chile? No, I have **never** been there.

How long ...?

Use this form to determine the period of time that an action lasted.

How long has Ms. Malone been the mayor? She has been the mayor for six years.

How many (times) ...?

Use this form to ask about the repetition of an activity.

How many times have you been to Portugal? I've been there twice.

TIP

Yet

Generally, use the present perfect with *yet*.

Has Jake left **yet**?

EXERCISE 6 WRITE QUESTIONS

Change the following sentences into questions. Answers to the questions are in bold.

EXAMPLE: **No,** I have never met her.
Have you ever met her?

1. Dr. Aboud has tested **hundreds** of children.
How many children has Dr. Aboud tested?

→

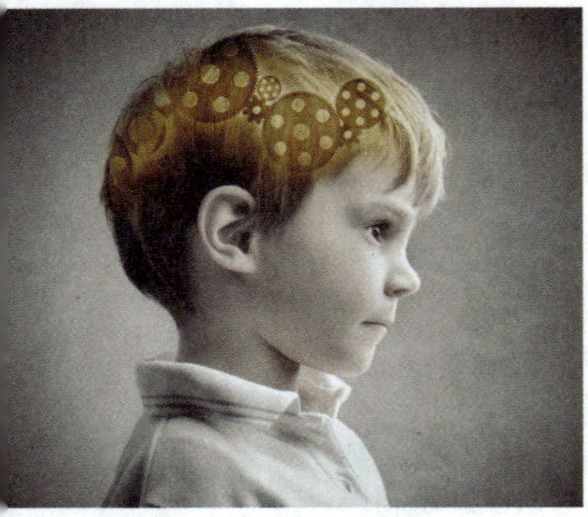

2. She has worked with that child **for three years**.
How long has she worked with that child?

3. **No**, she has never lived in the United States.
Has she ever lived in the United States?

4. She has published **more than forty** research papers.
How many research papers has she published?

5. **No**, she hasn't retired yet.
Has she retired yet?

EXERCISE 7 IDENTIFY ERRORS

Underline and correct the errors in the following sentences. Look for mistakes in verb tense or with the usage of *since* and *for*. Write C beside the sentences that are correct.

EXAMPLE: Have you ever saw a drone? (seen)

1. In 2001, New York's World Trade Center has collapsed. (collapsed)
2. According to journalist R. Fulford, the world changes a lot since 2001. (has changed)
3. Since then, North Americans had have a more militant attitude. (have had)
4. In June 2012, a pilotless remote-controlled aircraft has dropped a bomb on a house in Pakistan. (dropped)
5. Since the last few years, our society has become less tolerant. (For)
6. Fulford travelled to the United States many times. (has travelled)
7. Last March 9, he went through airport security. C
8. That day, security guards has searched his bags thoroughly. (searched)
9. Since 2001, people have change the ways that they communicate. (changed)
10. Smart-phone technology have improved since 2008. (has)
11. Since several years, I have used Skype to call my cousin. (For)
12. I buy many different cellphones over the years. (have bought)
13. How long you have had a phone? (have you had)
14. For three years, my brother owns an iPhone. (has owned)

EXERCISE 8 PAST, PRESENT PERFECT, AND PRESENT PERFECT PROGRESSIVE

Fill in the blanks with the past, present perfect, or present perfect progressive form of the verbs. (To review the present perfect progressive tense, see page 27.)

1. Christian (be) ___has been___ a war photographer for many years. He wants to publish a book of photographs. He (send) ___has sent___ proposals to several publishers. He (wait) ___has been waiting___ for a response for three months.

2. Another friend, Sun Hee, is also a photographer. She (take) ___has taken___ hundreds of amazing black-and-white portraits. Last week, she (decide) ___decided___ to publish a book about tolerance. She will try to sell it on Amazon. For the last six hours, she (work) ___has been working___ non-stop on her project, and her husband (sleep) ___has been sleeping___ because it is the middle of the night.

UNIT Review

Complete the following exercises. If you don't know an answer, go back and review the appropriate section.

1. When do you use the present perfect tense? Give two explanations.
   a) When a past action continues to the present time.
   b) When past actions occurred at unknown past times.

2. Underline and correct the verb-tense errors in the following sentences. Then write a rule to explain your corrections.
   a) Heather O'Neill has published her first book in 2006. ___published___
   Rule: Use the simple past when the past time of an action is known.
   b) Her book won many awards. ___has won___
   Rule: Use the present perfect when the time of past actions is unknown.
   c) She has been a famous writer since several years. ___for___
   Rule: Use *for* when referring to a quantity of years.
   d) She has wrote more than fifty poems. ___written___
   Rule: Use the past participle in the present perfect tense.
   e) For ten years, we have a dog. We love our dog. ___have had___
   Rule: Use the present perfect when an action begins in the past and continues to the present.

COMPANION WEB+ Need more practice? Visit the Companion Website and try more exercises on verb tenses.

Final Review

You can use the Final Review as a test. There are fifteen answers in Part A and five answers in Part B, for a total of twenty points. You can also find additional practice exercises and testing material on the Companion Website.

PART A

Fill in the blanks with the simple past or present perfect form of the verbs in parentheses.

EXAMPLE: I (see, never) have never seen a Muppets movie.

1. Filmmakers often create stereotypes because it is a simple way to establish a movie character's traits. For instance, the dumb blonde is a stereotype. During most of the last century, movie directors (care, not) did not care if their movies had racist elements. But for the last thirty years, most directors (try) have tried / have been trying to avoid stereotypical representations. However, someone will always dislike the choice of a movie's bad guy, who is often society's current villain. For instance, during World War II, movie villains were often German. In 2009, the directors of *The Muppets* (choose) chose the Texas oil tycoon, Tex Richman, as the villain. Ever since the film's release in 2011, the use of the "evil oil tycoon" character (cause) has caused some controversy.

2. In 2011, a popular news anchor from Fox Television (complain) complained bitterly about the Muppets movie. In fact, he (say) said that the movie was "pushing a dangerous liberal agenda and trying to brainwash children." Then, on April 2, 2012, a woman from Bee Cave, Texas, (phone) phoned Rush Limbaugh's radio show. During the call, she (yell) yelled about the movies *Cars* and *The Muppets*. Both films (sell) have sold a lot of tickets since their debuts. Holly, the Texan caller, said, "I (have) have had several bad experiences at the movies since the early 2000s. Over the last few years, my children (see) have seen some negative images of people who work in the oil industry. Many times, I (explain) have explained to them that their father's job isn't evil."

3. When the controversy first (begin) began, the producers of *The Muppets* were amused. In January 2012, the characters of Kermit the Frog and Miss Piggy (hold) ___held___ a news conference to defend their film. Since then, there (be) ___have been___ several funny YouTube videos about the incident.

PART B

Underline and correct the verb-tense errors in the following sentences. Write *C* beside the sentences that are correct.

4. In the early 1960s, Marilyn Monroe has been (was) one of Hollywood's most popular actresses.

5. Since the 1920s, hundreds of movies have include (included) the "dumb blonde."

6. During her lifetime, Marilyn Monroe hated her "dumb blonde" image and has tried (tried) to change it.

7. Since Monroe's death, biographers discovered (have discovered) that she was actually very intelligent.

8. Have you ever watch (watched) a Marilyn Monroe movie?

SPEAKING AND WRITING

Interview with a Famous Person

Work with a partner, and think about someone you both admire. It could be a well-known actor, scientist, athlete, musician, entrepreneur, or politician. After you have chosen someone, then imagine that you have the opportunity to interview that person. Write ten questions that you would ask him or her. Use a variety of verb tenses, and use the present perfect tense at least three times.

Students can do the writing exercise on a separate sheet of paper. Once they have finished, ask them to exchange their writing and peer edit for correct use of the present perfect tense.

UNIT 4 Past Perfect and Future Perfect Tenses

You can use the Preview activity to introduce the past perfect tense. Students can then complete the unit in class or for homework.

Preview

WHO DID IT?

Can you identify the differences between the simple past and the past perfect tenses? Read each group of sentences below and answer the questions that follow.

1. When the fire occurred, Mick had left the building.
   When the fire occurred, Rene left the building.
   Question: Who inhaled some smoke? Rene
2. When Tomas went to the London Olympics, he had won a gold medal.
   When Nicolas went to the London Olympics, he won a gold medal.
   Question: Who was already a gold-medal winner when he got to the London Olympics? Tomas
3. Last night at 9 p.m., Lia had taken her dog for a walk.
   Last night at 9 p.m., Jonathan took his dog for a walk.
   Question: Whose dog went for a walk before 9 p.m.? Lia's dog
4. Kendra had eaten when Gabriel invited her to dinner.
   Sara ate when Gabriel invited her to dinner.
   Question: Who was not hungry when Gabriel invited her to dinner? Kendra

Past Perfect Tenses: Forms and Usage

PAST PERFECT

The past perfect tense indicates that one past action happened before another past action.

The movie **had** already **started** when Jasmine arrived.

Past — The movie started. — Jasmine arrived. — **Now**

Keywords: already, up to that time, by then ...

PAST PERFECT PROGRESSIVE

The past perfect progressive indicates that an action was in progress (without interruption) before another past action occurred.

When I returned home, I realized that somebody **had been using** my computer. It was still warm.

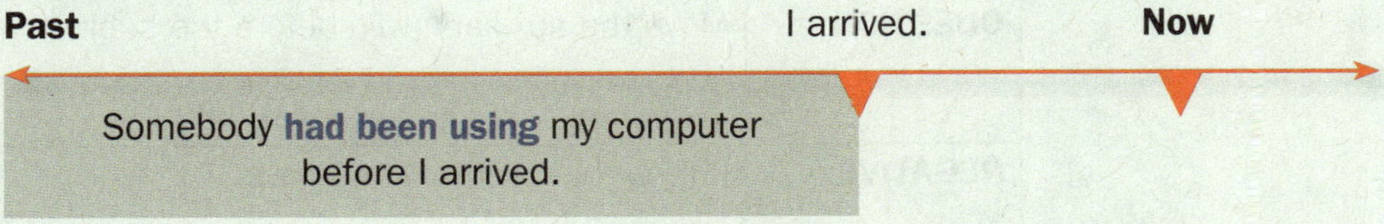

PAST PERFECT FORMS

FORM	Subject + *had* + past participle (eaten, seen, etc.) They **had completed** the project when I was hired.
QUESTION	Move the auxiliary (*had*) before the subject. What **had** she **done** before you arrived?
NEGATIVE	Add *not* after *had*. I **had not** (hadn't) **eaten** when the restaurant closed.
PROGRESSIVE	In the **past perfect progressive**, use *had been* + gerund (*-ing* form of the verb) to describe an action that had been continually in progress up to a specific past time. When I lost my job, I **had been working** at the company for ten years.

Note: When *before* or *after* is used in a sentence, the past perfect is not always necessary because the time relationship is already clear. Consider the following:

Past perfect: The movie **had ended**, so I left the theatre.

You could also use the simple past: After the movie **ended**, I left the theatre.

Future Perfect Tense: Forms and Usage

Use the future perfect tense to indicate that an action will occur before or up to a future time or future action.

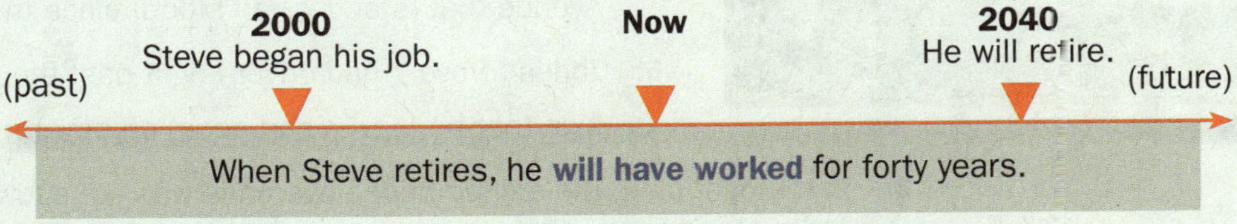

Keywords: by the time, by next year, by then, by Monday, by the weekend ...

FUTURE PERFECT FORMS

FORM	Subject + *will have* + past participle (gone, done, etc.) By next month, I **will have had** three operations.
QUESTION	Move the auxiliary (*will*) before the subject. How long **will** she **have worked**?
NEGATIVE	Put *not* between *will* and *have*. By next summer, I **will not** (won't) **have finished** my degree.
PROGRESSIVE	In the **future perfect progressive**, use *will have been* + *–ing* form of the verb to describe an action that will have been continually in progress up to a specific future time or action. When I retire, I **will have been working** for forty years.

Practice

EXERCISE 1 PAST AND PAST PERFECT

You might ask students to do this practice in pairs.

For each sentence, underline the correct form of the verb in parentheses.

EXAMPLE: When James Anthony Jones drove a group of students to George Washington's home, he (already worked / had already worked) as a bus driver for many years.

1. In 2004, bus driver James Anthony Jones had to drive a group of students to George Washington's house, a trip he (made / had made) many times.
2. By the time Jones started driving, he felt angry because the lead driver in another bus (insulted / had insulted) him.
3. While driving, Jones (called / had called) his sister and told her that he (never liked / had never liked) the other driver.
4. En route, there (was / had been) a bridge on Alexandria Avenue that (stand / had stood) since the early 1930s.
5. Jones (drove / had driven) right past the large yellow warning sign that he (saw / had seen) on several previous occasions.
6. In the right lane, the arched bridge overpass was quite low, but in the centre lane, it (was / had been) high enough for a truck to pass under.
7. The lead bus (already moved / had already moved) to the middle lane when Jones (arrived / had arrived) at the bridge.

8. Jones's bus (smashed / had smashed) forcefully into the bridge, and the collision (destroyed / had destroyed) the roof of the bus.

9. Investigators determined that Jones (tried / had tried) to multi-task by driving and speaking on a cellphone at the same time.

10. Later, Jones told investigators that he (didn't see / hadn't seen) the bridge.

EXERCISE 2 **IDENTIFY TENSE ERRORS**

Underline and correct ten verb-tense errors. Look for errors in any tense.

described
EXAMPLE: Marcia called a journalist and then had described the accident.

1. On March 15, 2012, Yuzu Noda was ~~tour~~ touring Australia with two of her friends. They ~~have~~ had never been to Australia before. At 11 a.m., they were driving beside a lake. Earlier, Noda had ~~program~~ programmed the destination of a nearby island into her GPS. When the GPS said, "Turn right," Noda ~~had turned~~ turned the wheel and drove into the lake. After the accident, Noda ~~was blaming~~ blamed her GPS. She argued that the machine had told her to turn. One of Noda's passengers later texted that she ~~was never~~ had never been so scared in her life.

2. Apparently, people often ~~are having~~ have accidents because they rely too much on their GPS devices. In another case, in June 2011, three women in Seattle were driving a Mercedes SUV that they ~~have~~ had rented. The car's GPS suggested that they turn onto a boat launch ramp, so the driver drove onto it. By the time the driver realized her error, the car ~~sunk~~ had sunk into the water. Of course, the woman had to pay an insurance penalty because she ~~has~~ had damaged the car.

PAST PERFECT PROGRESSIVE

Use the past perfect progressive to indicate that an action was in progress (without interruption) before another past action occurred.

It **had been raining** for about ten minutes when lightning struck the house.

EXERCISE 3 PAST FORMS

Fill in the blanks with the simple past, past progressive, past perfect, or past perfect progressive form of the verbs in parentheses, as appropriate.

EXAMPLE: When Wilson (arrive) <u>arrived</u>, Marino (cook) <u>had been cooking</u> for hours.

1. Last summer, when Art Wilson was in Venice, something strange (happen) ____happened____. He stopped in front of a small empty restaurant, and he could see an old woman who (cook) ____was cooking____ at the stove. She was stirring soup. Suddenly, he hād the feeling that he (be) ____had been____ there before. The shop owner, Rosina Marino, went outside because the strange man (look) ____had been looking____ at her for about five minutes. Wilson told her about his strong sense of déjà vu. He (feel) ____felt____ like he (be) ____had been____ there before, even though he (visit, never) ____had never visited____ Venice.

2. Marino and Wilson (talk) ____talked____ for a few minutes. Suddenly, they were thrown to the ground. The restaurant's gas stove (explode, just) ____had just exploded____. A few minutes earlier, Marino (stand) ____had been standing____ at that stove. Wilson never learned why he (have) ____had / had had____ that sense of déjà vu, but he was grateful that his feeling (save) ____had saved____ someone's life.

FUTURE PERFECT, PERFECT PROGRESSIVE, AND PROGRESSIVE

Use the **future perfect** to indicate that an action will occur before or up to a future time or future action.

The **future perfect progressive** shows that an action will be in progress up to a future time or action.

Future perfect:	Next summer, Zac **will have been** a student for exactly twenty years.
Future perfect progressive:	By Sunday, I **will have been working** for thirty hours non-stop on this project.

The **future progressive** indicates that an action will be in progress at a specific future time.

When you call me tomorrow, I **will be working**.

EXERCISE 4 **FUTURE PERFECT, PERFECT PROGRESSIVE, AND PROGRESSIVE FORMS**

Fill in the blanks with the future perfect, future perfect progressive, or future progressive form of the verbs in parentheses, as appropriate.

EXAMPLE: Tomorrow evening at 9 p.m., don't disturb me because I (study) will be studying. By next Tuesday, I (spend) will have spent three weeks preparing for the test.

1. I have a huge art project to do. It is 5 p.m., but I must finish it. Tonight at midnight, I (work, still) will still be working on it. I hope that I will finish by Sunday. Don't call me on Sunday. I'm planning to sleep all day. If you call at noon, I (sleep) will be sleeping. By the time I finish the project, I (spend) will have spent over eighty hours on it. When I finish my fine-arts degree next June, I (be) will have been a university student for four years.

2. On Monday, my sister is coming to visit. I work until 10:00 p.m., but my sister's bus arrives at 9 p.m. When I go to pick up my sister, her bus (arrive) will have arrived, and she (wait) will have been waiting for me for about an hour by the time I get there. But there is nothing I can do about it. She will have to wait.

UNIT Review

Complete the following exercises. If you don't know an answer, go back and review the appropriate section.

1. Underline three past perfect verbs and circle one future perfect verb.

were sleeping	had visited	have done	has seen	will have done
had tried	has gone	was	had had	will be doing

2. Underline and correct one error involving verb tense in each sentence.

a) When I arrived at the party, my hosts had already finish (finished) dinner.

b) Why they had (had they) already eaten?

c) I left the party and went to Maria's, but when I arrived at her house, she had went (gone) out.

d) Tonight, by the time I go to bed, I will be (have been) awake for twenty hours.

Need more practice? Visit the Companion Website and try additional exercises.

Final Review

You can use the Final Review as a test. There are twenty-five answers. You can also find additional practice exercises and testing material on the Companion Website.

Fill in the blanks with the appropriate form of the verbs in parentheses. You can use any form of the present, past, or future tenses.

EXAMPLE: In past centuries, kings and queens (have) had tremendous power.

1. These days in our history class, we (learn) are learning about ancient Egypt. So far, we (have) have had six quizzes. Tomorrow, when I (arrive) arrive in class, my professor will give us a two-hour exam on ancient Egypt.

2. In 55 BC, when the king of Egypt (die) died, the Egyptian people (expect) had expected / had been expecting his death for many months. A few days later, the king's seventeen-year-old daughter, Cleopatra, (become) became the queen of Egypt, and then she (marry) married her brother, Ptolemy, according to ancient tradition.

3. Three years later, when Julius Caesar (enter) entered Egypt, Ptolemy arranged a visit with the Roman ruler, but he excluded his sister. Cleopatra wanted to be a part of any deals, so she (plan) planned to meet Caesar too. She (hide) hid inside a rug and was delivered to Caesar's room.

4. Cleopatra (seduce) seduced Caesar. He told Cleopatra that he (see, never) had never seen such a beautiful woman. When he first (hear) heard her sing, he insisted that he (never, hear) had never heard such a sweet voice. That night, while the couple (whisper) were whispering in bed, Cleopatra (convince) convinced Caesar to make her the sole ruler of Egypt.

5. The next morning, Ptolemy arrived in Caesar's room and (realize) realized that Cleopatra (meet, already) had already met the foreign ruler. Ptolemy was furious and he (shout) shouted that his wife (spend) ___had spent___ the night with another man. Ptolemy then (threaten) ___threatened___ Caesar with revenge. In retaliation, Caesar (order) ___ordered___ Ptolemy's death. By the time Cleopatra and Caesar sailed for Rome, some guards (kill) ___had killed___ Ptolemy.

6. I (learn) ___have learned___ a lot about ancient Egypt since my course began. By the time we have our test tomorrow, I (study) ___will have studied / will have been studying___ for about twenty hours!

SPEAKING AND WRITING

Students can do the writing exercise on a separate sheet of paper. Once they have finished, ask them to exchange their writing and peer edit for correct use of verb tenses.

Life Lessons

Work with a partner. Read the next three sentences out loud, taking turns completing them. Try to speak without stopping, and then brainstorm to come up with as many ideas as possible for the three scenarios.

1. By the time I entered primary school, I had learned …
2. By the time I finished high school, I had learned …
3. By the time I finish college, I will have learned …

EXAMPLE: By the time I entered primary school, I had learned to tie my shoes. I had also learned to share. I had not yet learned to be a good loser.

When you finish, write a paragraph about your partner based on his or her responses to one of the scenarios.

UNIT 5

Adjectives and Adverbs

Use the Preview activity to introduce adjectives and adverbs. Then students can complete the unit in class or for homework.

Say each trait out loud and ask students to raise their right hand if it is a female trait and their left if it is a male trait. Then ask students to create sentences about the results. You can review comparative, superlative, and *as* ... *as* forms.

Preview

MEN AND WOMEN

The Implicit Association Test* assumes that people make connections between familiar pairs of ideas. For example, if we hear the name "Amanda," we automatically associate it with a woman.

PART A

Try the next test. Be spontaneous. Don't spend too much time thinking about your choice. Just put a check mark in either the right or the left column.

Female		Male
______	emotional	______
______	a good cook	______
______	a strict parent	______
______	a fun parent	______
______	likes to shop	______
______	a good driver	______
______	aggressive	______
______	worries about appearance	______
______	nags and complains	______
______	supports family financially	______
______	peaceful	______

PART B

Discuss gender stereotypes, and then write a paragraph about the perceived differences between men and women.

* The Implicit Association Test was developed by Anthony G. Greenwald, Mahzarin Banaji, Brian Nosek, and other social psychology researchers.

Adjectives and Adverbs: Forms and Usage

Adjectives describe nouns (people, places, and things) and pronouns (words that replace nouns). They add information explaining how many, what kind, or which one. They can appear before nouns or after linking verbs such as *be*, *look*, *appear*, and *seem*.

Before a noun: She is an **intelligent** and **beautiful** woman.

After a linking verb: He seems **serious**.

Adverbs are words (or groups of words) that add information to verbs, adjectives, and other adverbs. Most adverbs end in *–ly*, but there are some exceptions, such as *fast*, *often*, and *hard*.

He works **quickly**.

COMPARATIVE AND SUPERLATIVE FORMS OF ADJECTIVES AND ADVERBS

	ADJECTIVE OR ADVERB	COMPARATIVE	SUPERLATIVE
A. Add *–er* or *–est* to one-syllable adjectives.	short fast	short**er** than fast**er** than	the short**est** the fast**est**
When an adjective ends in a consonant-vowel-consonant, double the last letter.	hot	hot**ter** than	the hot**test**
B. In two-syllable adjectives ending in a consonant + *–y*, change the *–y* to *–i* and add *–er* (comparative form) or *–est* (superlative form).	easy funny	eas**ier** than funn**ier** than	the eas**iest** the funn**iest**
C. Add *more* (comparative form) or *most* (superlative form) to adjectives of two or more syllables and to compound adjectives.	modern well-liked	**more** modern than **more** well-liked than	the **most** modern the **most** well-liked
D. Add *more* (comparative form) or *most* (superlative form) to adverbs ending in *–ly*.	easily quickly	**more** easily than **more** quickly than	the **most** easily the **most** quickly
E. Some adjectives and adverbs have special comparative and superlative forms.	good / well bad / badly much / many little (a small amount) far	**better** than **worse** than **more** than **less** than **farther** / **further*** than	the **best** the **worst** the **most** the **least** the **farthest** / the **furthest***

* *Farther* indicates a physical distance. *Further* means "additional" and *furthest* means "to the greatest degree." For example: I need **further** information before I can make a decision.

EQUALITY: *AS ... AS / THE SAME AS*

Both *as ... as* and *the same as* express equality.

The thief is **as old as** my father.

He ran away **as fast as** he could.

That cellphone is **the same colour as** mine.

Sometimes one object is not as "equal" as another.

Knives are **not as dangerous as** guns.

Practice

EXERCISE 1 **COMPARATIVE AND SUPERLATIVE FORMS OF ADJECTIVES**

Write either the comparative or superlative forms of the adjectives in parentheses. Remember to also write *than* or *the*.

EXAMPLE: One of (old) the oldest crime movies is about John Dillinger.

1. Many movies make criminals' lives appear (exciting) more exciting than they really are. In movies, the criminals are (rich) richer than ordinary people. Their houses and cars are (good) better than those of ordinary people. They have (good) the best lives of all because they can work whenever they want and buy whatever they desire. But in the real world, a life in crime is (difficult) the most difficult life possible.

2. First, real-world criminals feel (guilty) guiltier than ordinary people. Their lives are (bad) worse than the lives of honest citizens. For instance, "Tim" sold cocaine in 2005, and one of his customers died. In an interview, Tim said, "My client had become a close friend. The day he died was (bad) the worst day of my life! I could no longer pretend that my work was not hurting anyone."

3. Also, it is not always easy to leave a life of crime. In most criminal syndicates, members must commit for life. Leaving a criminal gang is (dangerous) more dangerous than leaving any other job. Honest citizens are (lucky) luckier than criminals. Definitely, an honest life is (good) better than a life of crime.

TIP

***Than* or *Then*?**

In comparisons, use ***than***. Do not use ***then***, which means "next" or "after that."

The US has more prisons **than** ~~then~~ Canada does.

TWO-PART COMPARATIVES

Usually, you would use *the* in superlative rather than comparative forms. However, there are some two-part comparatives that require *the*. In these expressions, the second part is the result of the first part.

action — result

The more you exercise, **the better** you will feel.

Mention to students that sometimes the second part of a comparison is implied. For example, in Exercise 2, the fourth sentence really means "... money seldom makes people feel better **than they would feel without money**."

EXERCISE 2 IDENTIFY ERRORS

Underline and correct twelve errors involving comparative forms of adjectives, including incorrect spelling.

EXAMPLE: That is the most strange [strangest] information that I have ever heard.

1. The ~~more~~ greedier people are, the greatest [greater] the chance that they will commit a crime. Some individuals turn to crime because they want to be richest [richer] than before. They think that the most [more] they spend, the happiest [happier] they will be. However, money seldom makes people feel best [better]. In fact, when sociologists examined the ~~most~~ wealthiest Canadians, they discovered that their lives weren't better than the lives of their peers.

2. Generally, humans have a happiness set point. Often, after they gain a lot of money, they briefly feel ~~more~~ better. But after a couple of months, they return to their set point. Thus, they find new things to complain about, and sometimes their lives become worst [worse] than before. In a study, the extremely rich had higher drug-abuse rates then [than] others. Extreme wealth may be the less [least] important component of a person's happiness. In fact, the true indicator of happiness is personal relationships. The most [more] close relationships someone has, the better he or she will feel.

Draw attention to the spelling tip on page 50. Point out that words such as *really* and *finally* have a double *l*.

SPELLING OF ADVERBS

When a word ends in *–l*, form the adverb by adding *–ly*.

The team of historians worked **carefully**.

When a two-syllable word ends in *–y*, form the adverb by changing the *–y* to *–i* and adding *–ly*.

They worked together **happily**.

TIP

Irregular Adverbs

Some adverbs such as *often* never end in *–ly*.

EXERCISE 3 **ADVERBS**

Decide if each of the following sentences requires an adjective or an adverb. Then add *–ly* if necessary. If no *–ly* is required, put an *X* instead.

EXAMPLE: The robber acted *quick*_ly_.

1. Ken Leishman was *responsible*_X_ for a series of robberies in the 1950s and 1960s. He and his accomplices had to work very *quick*_ly_. In 1966, Leishman masterminded "the great gold heist," the largest theft of gold in Canadian history. After that crime, Leishman was *often*_X_ referred to as the "Flying Bandit."

2. Leishman thought *serious*_ly_ about the gold theft while he was in prison for an earlier crime. He came up with an *extreme*_ly_ risky plan. After he got out, he was *cautious*_X_, and he found accomplices to help do the crime. First, he *careful*_ly_ stencilled fake Air Canada logos on coveralls. He waited *patient*_ly_ until a clerk left an Air Canada desk, and then he stole some waybills, which are documents that give shipping instructions. His accomplices posed as airport security and, using a fake waybill, they *casual*_ly_ picked up the load of gold at the airport. The plan was *successful*_X_.

3. Leishman was eventually imprisoned for the heist. He *successful*_ly_ escaped from prison and stole an airplane. Authorities caught him and then released him again. In 1975, he moved to a *peaceful*_X_ town called Red Lake, Ontario. He lived there *quiet*_ly_ for four years. Later, in 1979, a plane he was flying *mysterious*_ly_ disappeared, reinforcing the myth of the "Flying Bandit." He was *official*_ly_ declared dead in 1980.

PLACEMENT OF FREQUENCY ADVERBS

Frequency adverbs—words such as *always*, *often*, *sometimes*, *usually*, and *ever*—indicate how often someone performs an action or how frequently an event occurs.

Place frequency adverbs before regular present and past tense verbs.

Police officers **sometimes** work at night.

Place frequency adverbs after the verb *be*.

The officer is **often** very busy.

Place frequency adverbs after auxiliary verbs.

She has **never** used her gun.

TIP

Real Versus *Really*

Real is an adjective that means "genuine" or "not fake."

He bought his girlfriend a **real** diamond.

Really is an adverb that means "in reality" or "actually." *Really* also expresses the degree to which something is true. **Note:** Never put *very* before a verb.

They worked **really** hard on the song.   They ~~very~~ **really** wanted attention.

Ensure that you always modify a verb using an adverb.

The protestors yelled ~~real loud~~ **really loudly** during the riot.

EXERCISE 4 **IDENTIFY ERRORS**

Underline and correct ten errors involving adjective and adverb forms and word order.

EXAMPLE: Newspapers and magazines contain often (often contain) articles about corruption.

1. Most cities have political corruption. Mayors must careful (carefully) deal with contractors for public works. Certain companies receive often (often receive) the most building contracts. They act real (really) suspiciously. Canadians, for instance, hear often (often hear) about corruption in the construction industry, and they very (really) want the government to take action. Politicians do not act quick (quickly) enough when there are allegations of corruption.

2. Citizens often are (are often) skeptical about the political system. They believe usually (usually believe) that all politicians are dishonest. Perhaps governments will eventualy (eventually) take action to stop corruption. I very (really) hope so.

TIP

As ... As

Remember to use *as ... as* when two items have equal value.

Brad is **as** guilty ~~than~~ **as** his brother.

EXERCISE 5 **ADJECTIVES AND ADVERBS**

Complete each sentence with the correct form of the word in parentheses. You may need to change an adjective to an adverb. You may also need to supply the following words: *than* or *as ... as*.

EXAMPLE: The judge speaks (loud) <u>more loudly than</u> the lawyer.

1. Countries have different legal systems and sentencing guidelines. For example, in the US, sentences are (strict) ___stricter than___ they are in Canada. Canadian prisoners usually get out of jail (quick) ___more quickly than___ American prisoners. The Canadian system is not the same as the American system; it's not (harsh) ___as harsh as___ the US system.

2. Certain prison guards attempt to be (nice) ___nicer___ to the criminals in their care than others do. Some guards treat prisoners (harsh) ___more harshly than___ others do. Certainly, guards earn (much money) ___more money than___ people in many other professions. Sometimes, they are not (compassionate) ___as compassionate as___ they could be. Perhaps they should receive (good training) ___better training than___ they currently receive.

3. Canadian prisoners are (lucky) ___luckier than___ the prisoners of many other countries. Canadian prisons generally meet international standards of safety and cleanliness, and prisoners are treated (humane) ___more humanely than___ prisoners in many other countries.

GOOD/WELL AND BAD/BADLY

Good is an adjective, and ***well*** is an adverb.

Adjective: They had a very **good** relationship.
Adverb: They communicated really **well**.

Exception: Use *well* to describe a person's health.

She is not **well**. She has the flu.

Bad is an adjective, and ***badly*** is an adverb.

Adjective: Yoko was not a **bad** singer.
Adverb: However, some critics reacted **badly** to her work.

EXERCISE 6 *GOOD, WELL, BAD, AND BADLY*

Underline the appropriate adjectives or adverbs in parentheses.

EXAMPLE: Some journalists write really (good / well).

When a major crime happens, the criminal (regular / regularly) receives more attention than the victim. In fact, some people commit crimes because they crave fame (bad / badly). They don't behave (good / well), yet they get a lot of attention. For example, the culprits in school shootings become (good / well) -known celebrities. The victims, who were (good / well) people, aren't remembered very (good / well). Perhaps the members of the media (bad / badly) need to change their focus. When a shooter opens fire on innocent people, his or her name should not be publicized. Criminals should not receive the attention that they want so (bad / badly). Perhaps (good / well) behaviour should be rewarded more than (bad / badly) behaviour.

FEWER VERSUS *LESS*

When you are comparing count nouns, use ***fewer*** or ***the fewest***. When you are comparing noncount nouns, use ***less*** or ***the least***. (For more information about noncount nouns, see Unit 8, page 77.)

Count noun: Blainville has **the fewest criminals** in Quebec.
Noncount noun: I have **less time** than you do.

Note: Use *less* and *the least* when another adjective appears before the noun.

Rene had **the least believable alibi**.

TIP

Adjective or Noun?

A noun may act like an adjective when it modifies another noun. Remember that adjectives are singular.

The shirt costs fifty **dollars**.	It is a fifty-**dollar** shirt.
(*Dollars* is a noun.)	(*Dollar* acts as an adjective and modifies *shirt*.)

EXERCISE 7 IDENTIFY ERRORS

Underline and correct errors involving adjectives or adverbs. Write *C* next to correct sentences.

simple person
EXAMPLE: He is a person simples.

dollar
1. A prison is a multi-million-dollars building. →

2. The average prisoner is a thirty-three-years-old man. year

3. Canada incarcerates less people than many other countries do. fewer

4. The average sentence for armed robbery is seven years-and-a-half. -and-a-half years

5. Regina is the less safe city in Canada. least

6. Crime movies are less realistic than other types of movies. C

7. Children are influenced more easier than adults are. easily

8. Sometimes children very hope to become criminals. really

9. After Rick committed a crime, he escaped as quickly than he could, but the police caught him. as

10. Rick's prison cell has no paper toilet. toilet paper

11. A typical school has fewer rules than a prison does. C

12. Mexico has the bigger crime problem in North America. biggest

13. Canadians have less guns than Americans do. fewer

14. Which country has the least problems? fewest

15. Most countries have real big problems with drug gangs. really

UNIT Review

Complete the following exercise. If you don't know an answer, go back and review the appropriate section.

Underline and correct the errors in the sentences below.

1. If you complain, it will make things worst than before. worse
2. Carol has as much money than I do. as
3. Bill is a more better businessman than Donald. ~~more~~
4. The harder you work, the worst you will feel. worse
5. Alex does the less amount of work of anyone that I know. least
6. Alex sings real good. really well
7. He feels bad about his situation. badly
8. the guards work often overtime. often work

COMPANION WEB+ Need more practice? Visit the Companion Website and try more grammar exercises.

Final Review

You can use the Final Review as a test. There are twelve answers in Part A and eight in Part B, for a total of twenty points. You can also find additional practice exercises and testing material on the Companion Website.

PART A

Write the correct comparative or superlative form of each word in parentheses. In some cases, you may need to change an adjective to an adverb. You may also need to add *the* or *than*. Do not use *as* ... *as*.

EXAMPLE: A sentencing circle is (good) <u>better than</u> a regular courtroom.

1. In past centuries, shaming penalties were very common. Judges ordered shaming penalties much (frequent) ___more frequently than___ they do today. One of (bad) ___the worst___ penalties involved the pillory. The wooden structure could lock a person's hands and head in place. The goal was to publicly humiliate the offender. Sometimes, even (nice) ___the nicest___ citizens in town would spit on the criminal. In addition, in the past, police officers were (powerful) ___more powerful than___ they are today. They could arrest people (easy) ___more easily than___ they can today. Nowadays, there are many protections for citizens.

2. Today, shaming penalties are rare, but they are coming back in fashion. For example, a judge in Wisconsin orders shoplifters to stand in front of the stores they robbed, holding a sign that reads, "I am a shoplifter." One shoplifter said the shaming was (bad) ___worse than___ jail. "All of my neighbours saw me. It was (sad) ___the saddest___ day of my life," said Reena King.

You can ask students to remove this page and hand it in. In the student books, pages are perforated.

3. Near Boston, when a ferry owner poured pollutants directly into the ocean, a passenger called the police. These days, ocean polluting is treated (severe) ___more severely than___ it was in the past. In court, the judge ordered the ferry owner to put a full-page ad in a Boston newspaper, reading, "Our company has discharged human waste into coastal waters." The ferry owner said that paying a fine is (easy) ___easier than___ facing public humiliation. For companies, bad publicity is (effective) ___the most effective___ type of punishment.

4. Some judges say that the shaming system works. Nowadays, people change their behaviour (quick) ___more quickly than___ they did in the past

You can ask students to remove this page and hand it in. Note that in the student books, pages are perforated.

because they realize they might face public humiliation. Many judges believe that public shaming is (good) ___the best___ penalty of all.

PART B

Underline and correct the errors involving adjectives or adverbs. Write *C* beside any sentence that is correct.

EXAMPLE: The thief was a <u>real</u> [really] greedy man.

5. Sam Rice did his ~~most~~ biggest crime in 2011.

6. The more Sam stole, the better he felt. C

7. He believed that he was the <u>less</u> [least] likely criminal in the city to get arrested.

8. Sam thought that he could blend in with the crowds really <u>good</u> [well].

9. But one day, he was not as careful as his accomplice was. C

10. In the end, his criminal skills were not as good <u>than</u> [as] he thought, and he ended up in prison.

11. These days, he has <u>less</u> [fewer] ideas about stealing than he did in the past.

12. Sam wants to change his life, and he doesn't want to behave <u>bad</u> [badly] anymore.

SPEAKING AND WRITING

Students can do the writing exercise on a separate sheet of paper. Once they have finished, ask them to exchange their writing and peer edit for correct use of comparative, superlative, and equal (*as ... as*) forms of adjectives and adverbs.

Crime and Consequences

Work with a partner, and then discuss one of the following topics. Then write sentences that use the comparative form, the superlative form, and the equal (*as ... as*) form of adjectives and adverbs.

1. Should youths be judged less harshly than adults are for crimes? Why or why not?
2. What are the best and worst punishments for prisoners?
3. Who gets more attention when a major crime happens: the criminal or the victim? Why?
4. Who commits more crime: males or females? Discuss why one gender is more likely to commit criminal acts.

UNIT 6

Modal Auxiliaries

Discuss the following e-mails with the class. Use the Preview activity to introduce modals.

Preview

LETTERS OF ADVICE

Work with a partner and read the following e-mails. Discuss what each letter writer should do. Then compose letters of advice to the writers.

My partner is an alcoholic. She promised to stop drinking when we got married, and I believed her. Now we've been married for a month, and she still drinks a lot of wine every day. About three times a week, she comes to bed completely drunk. Should I have married her? What should I have done when I learned that she is an alcoholic?
Anonymous

A few months ago, I discovered that my fourteen-year-old son was a hacker. After I got suspicious and checked his computer, I found a page showing people's credit card numbers and passwords. He promised to stop hacking, but he still seems to have a lot of money and doesn't tell me where it is from. I don't like to punish him, but I'm worried that he'll get into trouble. What mistakes have I made? What should I do now?
Sofia

Modal Auxiliaries: Forms and Usage

COMMON MODAL AUXILIARIES

FUNCTION	MODAL	EXAMPLE	PAST FORM
ability	**can**	I **can climb** mountains.	**could climb**
polite request (question form)	**may** **would** **could** **can**	**May** I **help** you? (formal) **Would** you **like** some coffee? **Could** you **open** the door? **Can** I **help** you? (informal)	
advice* opinion	**should** **ought to**	She **should see** a lawyer. The lawyer **ought to meet** her.	**should have seen** **ought to have met**
obligation	**must** **have to****	Now, the baby **must sleep**. Now, she **has to sleep**.	**had to sleep** (past form of both *must* and *have to*)
probability	**must**	Chantal **must be** tired.	**must have been**
possibility	**could** **might** **may**	The clerk **could help** you. I **might take** the job. Ann **may need** them.	**could have helped** **might have taken** **may have needed**
conditional action desire / preference past habit	**would** **would like** **would rather**	If I had time, I **would visit** her. (expresses a wish) I **would like** some coffee. I **would rather be** happy than rich. In my youth, I **would drive** for hours.	**would have visited** **would have liked** **would rather have been**

* You can use the form ***had better*** to indicate a strong recommendation.

You **had better hurry** or you'll miss the bus.

** Although *have to* is not a modal auxiliary, it is included here because it functions like a modal and has the same meaning as *must*. Its third-person-singular form is *has to*. For the past, use *had to*, and for the future, use *will have to*.

Practice

The Companion Website includes additional exercises.

Answers will vary.

EXERCISE 1 **MIXED MODALS**

Insert the appropriate modals in the blanks. The function of each modal is indicated in parentheses. In some cases, more than one answer is possible.

EXAMPLE: We (*advice:* leave) <u>should leave</u> now. It's getting late.

1. According to the BBC News, Britain is a "surveillance society." England has one security camera for every thirty people. Citizens (*advice:* drive, not) ___should not drive___ over the speed limit because speed cameras are on highways. Police (*ability:* give) ___can give___ really large fines

to people who speed. Cameras on telephone poles and storefronts (*possibility:* film) ___could / may / might film___ people who commit crimes.

2. Simon Davies, of the watchdog group Privacy International, believes he (*obligation:* speak) ___must speak / has to speak___ about Britain's increasing use of closed-circuit cameras. He points out that Britain has more surveillance cameras than China does. England (*possibility:* become) ___could / may / might become___ a police state. According to Davies, "In the past, we (*past ability:* walk) ___could walk___ on public streets without being filmed. Today, we (*obligation:* be) ___must be / have to be___ careful because we are all under surveillance." Davies thinks people (*advice:* protest) ___should protest___ about the issue.

MUST NOT VERSUS *DON'T HAVE TO*

Both *must* and *have to* indicate that something is necessary. However, the meanings are different in the negative form.

Must not means something is not permitted.

You **must not touch** that bomb. It is too dangerous!

Don't have to means there is no obligation, but you can do it if you want.

You **don't have to stay** here. You can leave.

EXERCISE 2 *MUST NOT* OR *DON'T HAVE TO*

Fill in the blanks with the negative form of either *must* or *have to*.

EXAMPLE: The children _must not_ touch the dog. He is very fierce.

1. In Canada, you ___must not___ carry a baby on your lap while driving. It is illegal.
2. In England, you ___must not___ drive on the right side of the road. The traffic laws are different, and everyone must drive on the left side of the road.
3. In English pubs, you ___don't have to___ tip the bartender. It isn't expected.
4. England has strict gun-control laws. You ___must not___ bring a firearm into the country. It is illegal.
5. Marley ___doesn't have to___ stay at a hotel. If he wants, he can stay with us.

PAST FORMS OF *MUST*

Must can indicate an obligation, but it can also mean that something is probable.

When *must* means "it is necessary," the past form is *had to.*

She **must leave** now. Yesterday, she **had to leave**.

When *must* means "it is probable," the past form is *must have* + the past participle.

He **must be** tired. Yesterday, he **must have been** tired.

EXERCISE 3 PAST FORMS OF *MUST*

Read the first sentence in each pair, and decide if *must* indicates a probability (*P*) or an obligation (*O*). Then complete the second sentence with the correct past form of *must* (*must* or *have to*).

EXAMPLE: There **must be** a problem with the engine. P

Past form: Yesterday, there must have been a problem with the engine.

1. Layla's new smart phone **must cost** a lot. P

   Past form: Layla's old cellphone must have cost a lot.

2. According to her contract, Layla **must pay** for Internet access on her phone. O

   Past form: Last year, Layla had to pay for Internet access on her phone.

3. Her phone is too large for her pocket, so she **must carry** it in her purse. O

   Past form: Her old phone was also large, so she had to carry it in her purse.

4. She lost her new phone. She **must be** upset. P

   Past form: Last year, she lost her phone. She must have been upset.

5. Layla fell and cut her hand, so she **must get** stitches. O

   Past form: Last month, she cut her foot, and she had to get stitches.

PAST FORMS OF *SHOULD*, *COULD*, AND *WOULD*

To form the past tense of modals such as *should*, *could*, and *would*, add *have* + the past participle.

Before Rosalie and Mark went to Panama, they **should have learned** a few words in Spanish. They **could have communicated** with the locals, and they **would have had** a better time.

EXERCISE 4 **PRESENT AND PAST MODALS**

Insert the appropriate modals in the blanks. In some cases, there may be more than one answer.

EXAMPLE: When he was a child, he (can, write) could write computer code.

1. Michael Calce was born in 1985 in Montreal. After his parents divorced, he (have to, go) ______ had to go ______ back and forth from his mother's house to his father's downtown condo. When he was six years old, his father gave him a computer. By the time he was a teenager, Michael (can, hack) ______ could hack ______ into very complex computer systems. Of course, he (must, use) ______ had to use ______ an alias when he hacked. In 2000, he chose the name MafiaBoy. At that time, he (should, know) ______ should have known ______ that the name was provocative.

2. At the age of fifteen, Calce carried out one of the first major computer hacks in the world. In 2000, companies such as CNN, Yahoo, Amazon, and Dell (have to, pay) ______ had to pay ______ a lot of money to repair the damage caused by Calce. They realized that they (should, prepare) ______ should have prepared ______ for cyber attacks at that time. They (must, be) ______ must have been ______ shocked that the perpetrator was a fifteen-year-old Canadian. From 2001 to 2005, Calce's actions (may, prompt) ______ may have prompted ______ many companies to improve their security systems.

3. Today, companies (can, spend) ______ can spend ______ millions of dollars making sure their computer systems are secure. Still, the possibility exists that another teenager (might, infiltrate) ______ might infiltrate ______ the website or data of a major corporation. Back when I was in university, I probably (should, study) ______ should have studied ______ computer science. Then I (would, find) ______ would have found ______ a better job when I graduated in 2006.

QUESTION FORMS

In question forms, move the modal auxiliary before the subject.

They **can** dance well.	**Can** they dance well?
He **should** have helped.	**Should** he have helped?

Exception: *Have to*

Remember that *have to* is actually a regular verb, so you need to add *do*, *does*, or *did* to question forms.

Bruno **has to** work late.	**Does** Bruno **have to** work late?

If students make mistakes on sentences 3 and 5, point out that these are subject questions. The rule about subject questions appears in Unit 2.

EXERCISE 5 QUESTIONS WITH MODALS

Write questions for the sentences below. The answers to the questions are in bold.

EXAMPLE: We should go **to Toronto** next summer.
Where should we go next summer?

1. **Yes**, we can participate in the flash mob.
   Can we participate in the flash mob?
2. We should bring **pillows**.
   What should we bring?
3. **International Pillow Fight Day** might occur in Montreal.
   What might occur in Montreal?
4. News about this event can spread **through social networking sites**.
   How can news about this event spread?
5. **Last year's Toronto event** must have been fun.
   What must have been fun?
6. Chantal had to leave early **because she didn't have a pillow with her**.
   Why did Chantal have to leave early?
7. She should have brought **a pillow** to the flash-mob event.
   What should she have brought to the flash-mob event?
8. This year's event could last **about two hours**.
   How long could this year's event last?

NEVER WRITE *SHOULD OF*, *SHOULDA*, OR *GOTTA*

Should of* and *Shoulda

In spoken English, it sounds as if people are saying "should of" or "shoulda." These are non-standard forms, and you should avoid using them. Instead, for the past forms of *should*, *could*, and *would*, always include *have* + the past participle.

When Calce hacked computers, he ~~shoulda~~ **should have** known it was dangerous. Maybe his parents ~~would of~~ **would have** taken action.

Gotta

Similarly, *gotta* is not a standard word and should never be written. It is an incorrect contraction of *got* and *to*. In formal English, it is preferable to write and say *have to*, as in, "I have to leave." In informal English, you can also say, "I've got to leave."

I ~~gotta~~ **have to** buy a new laptop because mine stopped working.

EXERCISE 6 **IDENTIFY MODAL ERRORS**

Underline and correct ten errors involving modal forms.

EXAMPLE: Reena <u>shoulda</u> (should have) changed her password.

1. Last month, Reena took a short break from work. She <u>coulda</u> (could have) stayed home, but instead her boyfriend invited her to his parents' country house. One Tuesday morning, they set out on their trip. Reena was texting when she drove into a fence. Luckily, they weren't hurt, but they could <u>of</u> (have) had serious injuries. She should have <u>pull</u> (pulled) over to the side of the road before writing a text message.

2. Reena had to <u>stayed</u> (stay) in contact with her workplace, so she brought along her laptop. One morning, she went to buy food. The grocery store was crowded, so she <u>can't</u> (couldn't) finish her shopping quickly and she spent about two hours in the store. While she was shopping, Reena's boyfriend used her computer. Reena shouldn't <u>of</u> (have) told him the password. He went online and read Reena's e-mails and chat logs. He definitely <u>would seen</u> (would have seen) comments that she had made about him. When Reena realized what he had done, she <u>shoulda</u> (should have) yelled at him, but she didn't want to embarrass him in front of his parents. Reena's boyfriend claims that anyone <u>woulda</u> (would have) done what he did. Reena disagrees and argues that people <u>gotta</u> (have to) respect each other's privacy. Who do you agree with?

UNIT Review

Complete the following exercises. If you don't know an answer, go back and review the appropriate section.

1. Write the past form of each modal verb in bold.
   a) Amber **must go** home. had to go
   b) She **can write** computer programs. could write
   c) He **should change** his password. should have changed
   d) We **have to leave**. had to leave

→

2. Underline and correct the errors involving modal forms in the following sentences.

EXAMPLE: I coulda helped you yesterday. could have

a) You should've went to Calgary. gone

b) I really gotta find a better job. have to

c) When I was a child, I can ran really fast. could run

d) He must of been with his father yesterday. have

Final Review

You can use the Final Review as a test. There are fifteen answers. You can also find additional practice exercises and testing material on the Companion Website.

Underline and correct fifteen errors involving modal forms, including the use of *gotta*.

EXAMPLE: Maybe Sabu coulda [could have] saved himself.

1. I gotta [have to] tell you about some hackers associated with the Anonymous group. In 2011, a small group of hackers known as LulzSec decided that they would taking [take] down the CIA website. They also decided to hack the FBI. They were confident that nobody can [could] find out who they were. But those hackers shouldn't had [have] been so cocky. By May 2011, FBI agents knew that they had to found [find] LulzSec.

This exercise may be difficult to correct. Suggestion: Ask students to do this activity in pairs, and remind them to keep the modal forms. Then, you could assign the test in Unit 6 of the Companion Website.

Students can read more detailed information about these LulzSec hackers in the essay "Anonymous Strikes Back" on page 81 of *Avenues 3: English Skills*.

2. On June 7, 2011, two FBI agents put on their bulletproof vests and went to a housing complex in New York's Lower East Side. That day was sweltering, so the agents probably woulda [would have] been hot and sweaty. One agent knocked on the steel door at the home of Hector Xavier Monsegur, a twenty-eight-year-old unemployed father of two. Monsegur, who used the online name Sabu, can't [couldn't] believe it when he saw the agents. He knew that he gotta [had to] do something to save himself. In a plea bargain, Sabu agreed to work undercover and unmask

his co-hackers. Of course, he must <u>of</u> (have) felt really guilty, but he didn't want to lose his children and spend his life in prison.

3. In March 2012, two British citizens were arrested for being part of the group of hackers. Ryan Ackroyd, a twenty-five-year-old man, pretended to be a teen girl, Kayla, when he was online. He <u>shoulda</u> (should have) been more suspicious of Sabu. A few days later, Jake Davis, an eighteen-year-old hacker who used the name Topiary, was also arrested. He would <u>of</u> (have) been shocked when the police turned up at his door. Finally, in July 2012, TFlow, a sixteen-year-old male from London, was caught. None of them <u>can escaped</u> (could escape), and they were sent to jail. The larger Anonymous hacker community <u>must of</u> (must have) felt upset in 2012.

4. These days, Governments know that they <u>gotta</u> (have to) do something about computer hacking. Many believe that the four LulzSec hackers should not <u>attacked</u> (have attacked) government and corporate websites and that their arrest was justified. Others support the hackers. Of course, since then, other hackers have filled the void left by the arrests.

SPEAKING AND WRITING

Once each pair of students has finished the writing exercise, ask them to exchange their writing with another pair and peer edit for correct use of modals.

Regrets

Work with a partner and imagine the regrets that people in the following two situations feel. Explain what they could have done and should (or should not) have done. Then, on a piece of paper, write at least three sentences about each person's regrets. Give reasons for each statement.

SITUATION A

Taylor Greene, a financial advisor, convinced his friends and family members to unknowingly invest in fake companies. Greene spent the money and used new investors' money to pay older investors. Eventually, his scheme was discovered.

SITUATION B

During his six-year hacking career, Hector Xavier Monsegur started a group similar to Anonymous and he destroyed the reputations of many people. The FBI arrested him and convinced him to work undercover and expose other hackers. He agreed.

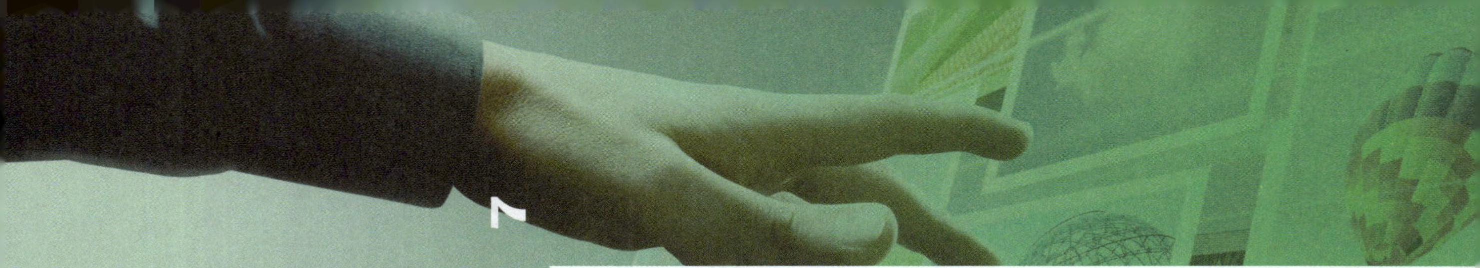

UNIT 7

Conditional Sentences

Use the Preview activity to introduce conditional sentences.

Preview

NON-STOP TALKING

Work with a partner or a small team and, one person at a time, speak non-stop about topic A, below. When the teacher flicks the light switch, change speakers. Repeat until all students have spoken, and then begin the exercise again, this time, speaking non-stop about topic B.

A. IF I COULD LIVE FOR 200 YEARS

Scientists are working hard to increase life expectancy. If you knew that you could live to be 200, how would your life change?

B. IF I HAD LIVED IN THE 1800s

Imagine what your life would have been like if you had lived in the 1800s. How would your life have been different?

Conditional Sentences: Forms and Usage

In conditional sentences, there are conditions and results. These types of sentences usually contain two clauses. The **main clause** depends on the condition set in the ***if* clause**. There are three conditional forms.

TYPES OF CONDITIONAL SENTENCES

1. **Possible Present or Future**

   Use this form when the condition is true or very possible.

Condition (*if* clause)		**Result**
If + present tense	→	present or future tense
If you **think** about it, (This present situation is true.)		life **is** fantastic.
If you **quit** your job, (This future situation is possible.)		you **won't be able to pay** the rent.

2. **Unlikely Present**

   Use this form when the condition is not likely and probably will not happen.

Condition (*if* clause)		**Result**
If + past tense	→	*would* (expresses a condition) *could* (expresses a possibility)

If I **won** money in a lottery, I **would build** a house.
(This condition is unlikely.)

If Eva **knew** how to speak Greek, she **could take** the job in Athens.

When the *if* clause contains *be*, always use *were*, even when the subject is *I*, *he*, *she*, or *it*. In informal speech, you may hear "was" in the *if* clause.

If I **were** rich, I **would buy** a new car.
If my sister **were** rich, she **would spend** a lot on clothing.

3. **Impossible Past**

Use this form when the condition cannot happen because the event is over.

Condition (*if* clause)		Result
If + past perfect tense	→	*would have* + past participle *could have* + past participle

If my grandfather **had won** money, he **would have given** it away.
If you **had told** me about the problem, I **could have stopped** the project.

MAKING A WISH

Wish about the Present

You make a wish when you want things to be different. When you **wish about a present situation**, use the past tense. When you **wish to change** a habit, use *would* or *could*.

I **wish** I **had** a great singing voice. (I can't sing, but I would like to.)
I **wish** you **would stop** smoking. (I wish you would change a habit.)

Wish about the Past

When you **wish you could change a past situation**, use the past perfect tense.

Leo **wishes** that he **had told** the truth to his wife.

Practice

EXERCISE 1 TYPES OF CONDITIONAL SENTENCES

Identify the types of conditional sentences. Write *A* (possible present or future), *B* (unlikely present), or *C* (impossible past) in the spaces provided.

EXAMPLE: If he gets the job, he will be really happy. A

1. If Jacob were older, he would apply for the job. B
2. If you want to learn about architecture, Jacob will teach you. A
3. If he had studied more, perhaps he would have passed all of his courses. C
4. Architecture is fascinating if you learn to appreciate it. A
5. He would design a new arena if the city hired him. B
6. If he had gone into the family business, he would have felt unfulfilled. C

EXERCISE 2 PRESENT AND PAST CONDITIONAL FORMS

Choose the correct form of each verb. Decide if the situation is possible or unlikely. Then use the possible present or future conditional form or the unlikely present conditional form.

EXAMPLE: If you play the scales every day, you (improve) <u>will improve</u> a lot.

1. James McCann has an unbelievable memory. If he looks at an image for about ten seconds, he (remember) <u>will remember / remembers</u> everything about it. This kind of memory is known as eidetic memory. If McCann (drive) <u>drove</u> down my street today, he would be able to detail every house, driveway, and hedge along the whole street. However, he probably won't visit my street.

2. McCann's memory is a fascinating subject for a psychology professor at his university. If the university (pay) <u>pays</u> McCann, he will let himself be tested for the sake of science. However, if the university (help, not) <u>doesn't help</u> financially, he will probably not consent to the study. McCann lives in Brisbane, Australia. If he (live) <u>lived</u> in Canada, he probably (enjoy, not) <u>wouldn't enjoy</u> the climate. Brisbane has a very nice climate.

EXERCISE 3 IMPOSSIBLE PAST CONDITIONAL FORMS

Complete the following sentences using the impossible past conditional form of the verbs in parentheses.

EXAMPLE: If the police (conduct) <u>had conducted</u> an investigation, they would have solved the case.

1. Is hacking ethical? Mark Ward, in *A Brief History of Hacking*, says that in the past "hackers were benign creatures." A "hack" was "an inspired solution to a problem." If you (live) <u>had lived</u> in the 1980s, you (admire) <u>would have admired</u> hackers. Most early hackers just wanted to find the flaws in computer systems. Some of them played silly pranks. For instance, Steve Jobs hacked into telephone systems to make free phone calls. Perhaps if the police (arrest) <u>had arrested</u> Jobs back in the 1980s, he (create, not) <u>would not have created</u> Apple Computer.

2. Another early hacker went by the name Dark Dante. He took over the phone lines when radio shows had contests, and as a result won major prizes. For instance, in 1990, when a Los Angeles radio show announced that the 102nd

caller would win a prize, Dark Dante used his hacking skills to ensure that he was the 102nd caller, so he won a Porsche. If those radio stations (know) ___had known___ their phone lines were being hacked, they (change) ___would have changed___ their contest rules. After such exploits became well-known, new anti-hacking laws were introduced.

EXERCISE 4 CONDITIONAL VERBS

For the following sentences, write the correct conditional form of each verb in parentheses.

EXAMPLE: If he (live) <u>had lived</u> in an earlier era, Mark Zuckerberg would not have created Facebook.

Mark Zuckerberg

1. If you do research on the Internet, you (learn) ___will learn___ a lot about Mark Zuckerberg. In 2002, the then-eighteen-year-old man wrote a computer program called Synapse. Bill Gates heard about Synapse. If Mark Zuckerberg (want) ___had wanted___ a job at Microsoft, he could have had one. Instead, he decided to stay at Harvard. For sure, if he (accept) ___had accepted___ the Microsoft job offer, his life (be) ___would have been___ different. If he had left Harvard, he probably (think, never) ___would never have thought___ about a college-based social networking site.

2. The following year, at Harvard, twins Cameron and Tyler Winklevoss asked Zuckerberg to help them write the programming code for a site called Harvard Connection. If Zuckerberg (refuse) ___had refused___ to help the twins, he (save) ___would have saved___ himself a lot of problems. But Zuckerberg agreed to help them, and then he quickly abandoned the project. Instead, in his dorm room, Zuckerberg built his own social networking site. This early version of Facebook was an immediate hit. At the end of the year, Zuckerberg dropped out of Harvard to run his site. He made the right decision. If he (stay) ___had stayed___ at Harvard, it's likely that Facebook (be) ___would have been___ less successful.

3. Back in 2003, if the Winklevoss twins (give) ___had given___ Zuckerberg a written contract, they (share) ___would have shared___ more fully in Facebook's profits. Today, the Winklevoss twins believe that Zuckerberg was unethical. But Zuckerberg argues that Facebook was original and was not similar to Harvard Connection. If I (be) ___were___ →

Zuckerberg, maybe I would feel the same way. Unfortunately, I don't know how to build websites. But if I (know) ___knew___ how to do it, I certainly (try) ___would try___ to come up with a great idea for a website.

> **AVOIDING PROBLEMS WITH THE PAST CONDITIONAL**
>
> In **impossible past conditional** sentences, the writer expresses a wish that a past event had worked out differently. Avoid the following common errors.
>
> Do not use *would have* or *could have* in the *if* clause. Use the past perfect tense instead.
>
> **had asked**
> If you ~~would have asked~~ me, I would have travelled with you.
>
> Do not write *woulda / coulda* or *would of / could of*, as they are non-standard forms. When you use the past forms of *would* and *could*, always include *have* + the past participle.
>
> **have**
> If you had done your homework, you would ~~of~~ passed the course.

EXERCISE 5 **IDENTIFY ERRORS**

Underline and correct twelve errors involving conditional forms in the following sentences.

EXAMPLE: If you had met Anna Chapman, you woulda [would have] liked her.

1. On a warm June day in 2010, Anna Chapman was sitting in a Manhattan coffee shop. If the shop would have [had] had free Wi-Fi, the Facebook addict would have check [checked] her Facebook page. However, the shop didn't offer free Internet access. If you woulda [had] seen Chapman that day, you woulda [would have] smiled. She looked like the girl next door, but the perky redhead was actually an undercover Russian spy.

Anna Chapman

2. Chapman's guest arrived. The good-looking man said he was working for the Russian consulate. In fact, he was an FBI agent. He offered Chapman a deal. She would earn a lot of money if she delivers [delivered] a fake passport to another Russian spy. Perhaps if Chapman would have [had] been more suspicious, she would have stayed out of trouble. But she agreed to do the transfer. If I was [had been] there, I would have warned her to be more careful. Soon after, Chapman and nine other Russian spies were arrested.

3. Normally, if someone betrays his or her nation, that person would go (goes / will go) to prison. However, the US and Russia didn't want to damage their relationship. High-ranking politicians decided that they would make a deal if it is (were) possible. In the end, America returned the ten spies to Russia and received four prisoners in exchange. If this deal had favoured the Russians, the US probably would not agree (have agreed) to it. It was actually better for the Americans. The four Americans in Russia had given extremely important information to Western nations before they were caught. The ten Russian spies, however, were "rank amateurs" according to the London newspaper the *Daily Mirror*. If Chapman wouldn't have (hadn't) been a spy, she could have stay (stayed) in America. Instead, she can never return to North America.

EXERCISE 6 WISHING AND CONDITIONAL FORMS

Point out that one of the options for the second answer in the first paragraph is *wouldn't call*, which implies that Clay wants his girlfriend to change a bad habit.

Complete the sentences using the correct form of the verbs in parentheses. To review information about making a wish, see page 67.

EXAMPLE: I wish I (know) knew the answer now, but I don't.

1. Clay is always busy. He works part-time and attends law school. These days, he wishes that he (have) ___had___ more time for a social life, but his studies are very demanding. He has a new girlfriend, and she is very needy. Clay wishes that she (call, not) ___wouldn't call / didn't call___ so often. Last year, Clay broke up with his previous girlfriend, Jaden. Now he wishes that he (leave, not) ___had not left___ her. He wishes that he (stay) ___had stayed___ with Jaden, but it is too late. She has a new boyfriend.

2. Clay doesn't enjoy his university program. He has spoken with several lawyers who wish they (choose) ___had chosen___ another field. They warned Clay that most jobs related to law are not very glamorous or well-paid. One lawyer named Marcus said, "I don't enjoy my job. I wish I (know) ___had known___ about the long hours when I was still a student. I would never have become a lawyer."

3. Clay often wishes that he (take) ___had taken___ a computer-related program instead of switching to law after his undergraduate degree. He wishes that he (think) ___had thought___ more about his future.

These are general rules for *hope* and *wish*; there are also many exceptions and nuances. For instance, people also use *hope* to express future plans, as in, "I hope to visit Spain next summer." And people also use *wish* to express a sentiment, as in, "I wish you good luck," or, "I wish you a merry Christmas."

THE DIFFERENCE BETWEEN *HOPE* AND *WISH*

Use ***hope*** when you want something to happen, but are not sure that it will (or did) happen.

I **hope** Joan's boyfriend **is** a nice guy.	(I am not sure that he is nice.)
I **hope** that I **pass** this course.	(I don't know if I will pass the course.)
I **hope** my brother **found** his car keys.	(I don't know if he found them.)

Use ***wish*** when you want to alter a present or past situation. People usually wish for improbable or unlikely things. Keep in mind that changing a past situation is *impossible*).

I **wish** that I **had** more money.	(I wish that I could change my present reality.)
I **wish** he **would stop** smoking.	(I wish that he would change his bad habit.)
I **wish** I **had met** Jacob.	(I wish that I could change a past event.)

TIP

Hope or Wish

To express a desire about a situation that was, is, or might be possible, use ***hope***. Don't use ***wish*** with the present tense.

hope
I ~~wish~~ I finish this project soon. I **wish** I had more time to work on it.

EXERCISE 7 ***HOPE* OR *WISH***

Fill in the blanks with *hope* or *wish*, as appropriate.

EXAMPLE: I _hope_ the bank is still open.

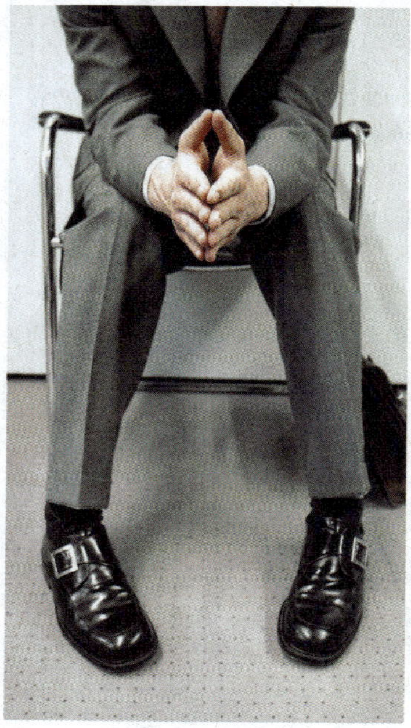

1. I am looking for an apartment. I ______hope______ I can find a place that's close to school. I ______wish______ I could afford to live in a bigger apartment.
2. Next week, I have a job interview. I ______hope______ that I will be hired. I ______wish______ I had more experience to put on my CV, but I have only had one job. I ______hope______ I'm able to charm the interviewer. I have been preparing for days. I ______wish______ I knew someone at the company because that could help my chances.
3. My father is coming to visit tomorrow. I ______hope______ he has something to do while he's here. I ______wish______ I could spend more time with him, and I ______hope______ he understands that I don't mean to be rude, but I have a lot of studying to do.

EXERCISE 8 IDENTIFY ERRORS

Answers may vary.

Underline and correct eight errors involving conditional verb forms and the incorrect usage of *hope* or *wish*.

EXAMPLE: Many people wish that there is [were] more sites like WikiLeaks.

1. In 2006, Julian Assange founded WikiLeaks. Then, in 2010, WikiLeaks published the content of a lot of sensitive diplomatic cables and documents. The documents embarrassed government officials in many nations. Those government workers probably wish that WikiLeaks kept [had kept] the documents secret. For example, US politician Hillary Clinton wishes that people didn't [hadn't] read embarrassing comments about her.

2. In 2010, Bradley Manning, a US soldier, was arrested for supplying secret documents to WikiLeaks. Today, Manning is in prison, and he's serving a life sentence. He probably wishes that he didn't pass [hadn't passed] along those documents. He probably also wishes that he thought [had thought] more about the consequences of his actions. Manning's supporters hope that he would [will] be released from prison soon. Certainly, if he would have [had] resisted the urge to send those documents to WikiLeaks, he would be a free man today.

3. I wish I knew [had known] about WikiLeaks when it was first launched. I think whistle-blower websites are fascinating. I wish [hope] that such sites always exist.

UNIT Review

Complete the following exercises. If you don't know an answer, go back and review the appropriate section.

1. For each sentence, write the verb *buy* in the correct tense form.
   a) I ___will buy___ it if I save enough money.
   b) I ___would buy___ it if I had a better job.
   c) I ___would have bought___ it if I had known what a great deal it was.

2. Underline and correct the verb tense error in each sentence.
   a) If I would be [were] younger, I would move to New York.

→

COMPANION Web+ Need more practice? Visit the Companion Website and try more grammar exercises.

b) If the public ~~would have~~ had known about Senator Klee's problems, they would have voted against him.

c) Soon Yi wishes that she ~~has~~ had more money.

d) If Soon Yi ~~were~~ had been at the rally, she would have helped Senator Klee.

Final Review

PART A

Write the correct form of the verbs in parentheses.

EXAMPLE: If the police (conduct) <u>had conducted</u> an investigation, the case would have been solved.

1. In the early 2000s, the British tabloid *News of the World* hacked into the cellphones of celebrities. Journalists used the information they uncovered to write gossipy stories. The public was not very interested. Perhaps if people (show) <u>had shown</u> more concern, the hacking (stop) <u>would have stopped</u> sooner. Unfortunately, people expect celebrities to have no privacy. For instance, if somebody (listen) <u>listened</u> to actress Jennifer Lawrence's phone messages, nobody would worry about it. If a magazine published a celebrity's private phone messages, a lot of people (read) <u>would read</u> the article.

2. In 2011, everything changed for *News of the World*. A lawyer announced that nine years earlier, journalists had hired hackers to access the cellphone of a thirteen-year old murder victim, Milly Dowler, and that some of her voice-mail messages had been deleted after the hackers had listened to them. Journalists wrote that if *News of the World* hackers (leave) <u>had left</u> Dowler's phone alone, police (spend) <u>would / could have spent</u> more time on the case. Because her messages had been deleted, police and family members assumed that she was still alive. Perhaps if the phone hackers

You can use the Final Review as a test. There are ten answers in Part A and five answers in Part B for a total of fifteen points. You can also find additional practice exercises and testing material on the Companion Website.

(consider) ______ had considered ______ the family's feelings, they (act) ______ would have acted ______ differently.

3. If *News of the World* employees had hacked into the phones of celebrities only, perhaps the publication (avoid) ______ would have avoided ______ closer scrutiny. But because they hacked into the phones of ordinary people, citizens were outraged. Rupert Murdoch had to shut down *News of the World* in the summer of 2011 because of the scandal. If the editors had acted responsibly, the newspaper (survive) ______ could have survived ______.

The first answer in question 4 could be "If I worked hard, I would succeed."

PART B

Underline and correct five errors involving conditional forms of verbs.

4. I want to be a journalist. If I worked [work] hard, I will succeed. Last year, I planned to enter a writing contest, but I didn't finish my essay in time. I wish I entered [had entered] the contest because the prize was $1000. Maybe if I would have [had] entered the contest, I would have won.

5. If one person owned all of Canada's newspapers, will [would] there be a problem? In fact, most of Canada's media outlets are controlled by only a few companies. In 1990, over 17 percent of Canadian newspapers were independently owned. By 2005, that number had dropped to 1 percent. Maybe if Canada had had better anti-monopoly laws, that wouldn't of [have] happened. Media consolidation can be dangerous because a few individuals can control what the public learns.

SPEAKING AND WRITING

Once students have finished the writing exercise, ask them to exchange their writing with their partner and peer edit for correct use of conditional sentences, including the correct use of *hope* and *wish*.

If ...

Discuss the following situations with a partner. Then, on a separate sheet of paper, create sentences explaining how you feel about each situation.

1. If you could have a special talent, what type of talent would you like to have?
2. If your parents had had a billion dollars, how would your childhood have been different?
3. Which celebrity do you wish you had met before he or she died? If you had met that person, what would you have said? (Examples: Mahatma Gandhi, Amy Winehouse, Napoleon, Pancho Villa, etc.)
4. What two things do you wish you had done in the past?

UNIT 8 Nouns, Determiners, and Pronouns

You can use the Preview activity to introduce nouns, determiners, and pronouns. Students can then complete the unit in class or for homework.

Preview

Work with a partner to identify and correct twelve mistakes in the following paragraph.

In 1989, Kalle Lasn and Bill Schmalz started a new medias [media] foundation. At first, they had very few [little] informations [information] about the magazine market, but they forged ahead and produced a popular magazine and website. Today, much [many] peoples [people] with all type [types] of lifestyles subscribe to *Adbusters*. In fact, it has more than ten thousands [thousand] subscribers. Two years ago, my parents gave a subscription to the magazine to my brother and I [me]. Many contributor [contributors] to the magazine have created amusing spoofs [spoof] ads. For example, last year, someone mocked a Joe Camel cigarette advertisement. The ad depicts "Joe Chemo" in a hospital bed. This [These] days, my brother and me [I] read that magazine every month.

Nouns, Determiners, and Pronouns: Forms and Usage

NOUNS

Nouns are words that refer to people, places, and things. Most nouns have both singular and plural forms.

SPELLING OF PLURAL FORMS

	SINGULAR	PLURAL
Most plural nouns simply end in *–s*.	student	students
Add *–es* to nouns ending in *–s*, *–ch*, *–sh*, *–x*, or *–z*.	match tax	matches taxes
When nouns end in *–f* or *–fe*, change the *–f* or *–fe* to *–v* and add *–es*. **Exception:** *beliefs*	shelf knife wife	shelves knives wives
When nouns end in a consonant + *–y*, change the *–y* to *–ies*.	berry spy	berries spies
When nouns end in a vowel + *–y*, just add *–s*.	day	days
When nouns end in *–o*, they may require an *–s* or an *–es* ending. Consult your dictionary if you're not sure which ending to use.	photo logo hero	photos logos heroes
Some nouns have **irregular plural forms.**	man child	**men** **children**
Some nouns are borrowed from **foreign languages**, so they keep the plural form of the original language.	analysis bacterium paparazzo phenomenon	analyses bacteria paparazzi phenomena

NOUNS THAT HAVE PLURAL FORMS ONLY

Some nouns appear in the plural form only. The objects or ideas might have two or more parts but are considered singular entities. Use plural verbs with these nouns.

binoculars	credentials	goods	scissors
clothes	(eye)glasses	savings	shorts

My **pants** are in the wash. My **glasses** are on the table.

PLURAL NOUNS WITH SINGULAR MEANINGS

Some nouns always have plural forms but singular meanings. Use third-person-singular verbs with these nouns.

economics	mathematics	mechanics
news	politics	physics

Physics is a difficult subject. The **news** appears online.

COUNT AND NONCOUNT NOUNS

Count nouns refer to people, places, and things that you can count, such as *girl* or *toy*. Count nouns have both singular and plural forms. **Noncount nouns** cannot be counted and have only singular forms.

Count: I own a **cellphone**. My brother has two **cellphones**.
Noncount: We have too much **homework**. **Money** changes people.

To express the quantity of a noncount noun, we use expressions that describe amounts, such as *types of*, *a lot of*, or *pieces of*. Note that the noncount noun remains singular.

pieces of information
I have two ~~informations~~.

Common Noncount Nouns

CATEGORIES OF OBJECTS		FOOD	NATURE AND SUBSTANCES	ABSTRACT NOUNS	
baggage	machinery	bread	air	advice	knowledge
clothing	mail	cheese	chalk	attention	luck
equipment	makeup	fish	coal	behaviour	patience
furniture	money	honey	electricity	education	publicity
homework	music	meat	fur	effort	proof
housework	postage	milk	hair	evidence	research
ink	software	rice	paint	health	time**
jewellery	wildlife	salt	radiation	help	trouble
luggage	work*	sugar	weather	information	violence

* *Work* is a noncount noun except when it refers to artistic works.
** *Time* is a noncount noun when it refers to free time or spare time.

DETERMINERS

DETERMINERS WITH COUNT AND NONCOUNT NOUNS

COUNT NOUNS (*many, few, a few*)	NONCOUNT NOUNS (*much, little, a little*)	COUNT AND NONCOUNT NOUNS (*a lot of*)
She has **very few*** friends. She has **a few**** friends. He has **many** friends.	She has **very little*** money. She has **a little**** money. He doesn't have **much***** money.	He has **a lot of***** friends and **a lot of** money.

* *Few* and *little* mean "almost none" and often indicate complaints.
** *A few* and *a little* mean "a small amount." There is no negative connotation.
*** Use *much* only in negative and question forms. In affirmative forms, use *a lot of* instead.

USING *THIS*, *THAT*, *THESE*, AND *THOSE*

TERM	USAGE	EXAMPLE
this (singular) **these** (plural)	Refers to things that are near the speaker in time or place.	**This** is a great summer. **These** days, it is sunny. **These** sunglasses that I'm wearing will protect me from UV rays.
that (singular) **those** (plural)	Refers to things that are far from the speaker in time or place.	Do you see **those** people in **that** store? In 2011, there were severe floods, so **that** was a difficult year.

PRONOUNS

Pronouns replace nouns, other pronouns, and noun phrases. A complete list of pronouns appears in *Avenues 3: Grammar Review Guide.*

SUBJECT PRONOUNS AND OBJECT PRONOUNS

A **subject pronoun** does the action and is usually followed by a verb. An **object pronoun** is affected by the action and is usually found after a verb or preposition. A sentence may have more than one subject or object.

subject pronoun — **She**; object pronoun — **them**; object pronoun — **it**

<u>The professor</u> talked to the <u>students</u> about <u>her latest experiment</u>.

subject — object — object

POSSESSIVE ADJECTIVES AND POSSESSIVE PRONOUNS

Possessive adjectives describe nouns and appear before the nouns that they describe. **Possessive pronouns** replace possessive adjectives and nouns.

Lola and Rick lost **their** (possessive adjective) passports. Did you lose **yours** (possessive pronoun)?

REFLEXIVE PRONOUNS

Use reflexive pronouns when the subjects doing the actions and the objects affected by the actions are the same people or things.

The small child dressed **herself**.
We helped **ourselves** to some coffee.

Practice

NOUNS: SPECIAL RULES

Each* and *Every

Use a singular noun after *each* and *every*.

Each **day**, Max cleans every **room** in his house.

One of the* and *Each of the

Use a plural noun after *one of the* and *each of the*.

That is one of the best **movies** I have ever seen! I love each of the **actors**.

Kind of, Sort of,* and *Type of

Always use the plural form of *kind of*, *sort of*, and *type of* when they refer to more than one kind, sort, or type. Also write the plural form of the noun that follows *of* unless it is a noncount noun.

There are many **kinds** of people in the world.
The store has several **types** of luggage. (*Luggage* is a noncount noun.)

TIP

Always Use Singular Forms of Adjectives

Adjectives have no plural form, so never add –s to adjectives.

There must be some ~~simples, plausibles~~ **simple, plausible** explanations.

Sometimes nouns act as adjectives.

I have eight **dollars**.
Dollar is a noun, and ends in –*s*.

She has a fifty-**dollar** shirt.
Dollar acts as an adjective, and does not end in –*s*.

EXERCISE 1 PLURALS

Using the spaces provided, change words to the plural form, if necessary. If no plural form is needed, write *X* instead. If the word ends in *–y,* you may have to first change the *–y* to *–i*.

EXAMPLE: There are many different recording compan~~y~~__ies__ in Canada.

1. Every day__X__, companies produce many type__s__ of new__X__ product__s__. One of the most important role__s__ of advertisers is to create brand__X__ identit~~y~~__ies__ that their customer__s__ will love. An interesting example__X__ involves the Canadian company Research In Motion (RIM). In 1999, Mike Lazaridis and Jim Balsillie formed the company. They were former mathematic__s__ and physic__s__ student__s__.
2. RIM's first product was the BlackBerry. Wireless mobile__X__ device__s__ could send a lot of information__X__ efficiently. The company soon made million__s__ of dollar__s__ selling the BlackBerry. Today, the company is worth about five billion__X__.* During the early 2000__s__, it was one of the fastest-growing compan~~y~~__ies__ in the world.

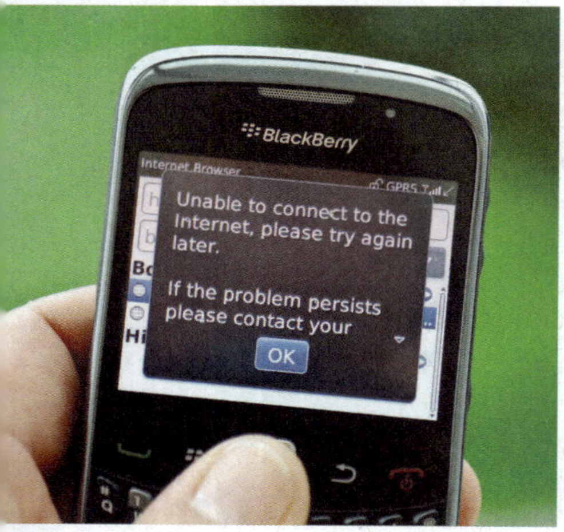

3. Since 2005, RIM has had a lot of severe__X__ problems. One of the major issue__s__ is a lack of vision. CEO Mike Lazaridis didn't listen to the advice__X__ he was getting from many employee__s__. In 2006, Steve Jobs created several__X__ successful promotional__X__ campaign__s__ for the iPhone. The iPhone had many kind__s__ of feature__s__ such as a camera__X__ and a lot of data__X__ storage. Lazaridis lost touch with what each consumer__X__ wanted from a cellphone. He thought people wanted the best-performing phone; he didn't realize he really needed to promote an image__X__.

COLLECTIVE NOUNS

Collective nouns such as *army*, *family*, and *association* refer to groups that act as units. Therefore, any pronoun that refers to a collective noun is singular. (A list of collective nouns appears on pages 2–3.)

The government will not revise ~~their~~ **its** policies.

* With monetary values, sometimes the word *dollars* is implied but not written. Thus, the word before *dollars* remains singular.

TIP

Media: Singular or Plural?

Technically, the word *media* is the plural form of *medium*. However, many newspapers, magazines, and websites treat media as a collective singular noun. Some experts believe that the singular usage will soon become the standard.

If you talk about social media as a **type of mass communication**, use the singular form.

Social **media** has influenced the way people exchange information.

If you want to treat social media as **various communication tools**, then use the plural verb form.

Social **media**—Facebook, LinkedIn, and Twitter—have changed our world.

Note: Never write "medias."

EXERCISE 2 **SINGULAR OR PLURAL NOUNS**

Decide if you want students to use the plural or singular form of *media*. Remind them never to write "medias."

Underline and correct fifteen errors involving plural forms in the following sentences.

EXAMPLE: The stores were filled with phones that were also musics [music] devices.

1. Most of us are obsessed with materials [material] items. We constantly read about new type [types] of gadget [gadgets] in the medias [media]. For example, we can read news storeys [stories] on different e-readers. People used to get their informations [information] from magazines or newspapers, but today, many can read the news on their smart phones. High-tech gadgets are a billion-dollars [dollar] industry.

2. These days, many peoples [people] think that a two-years-old [year] cellphone is useless. Most phones can now take better photoes [photos] than digital cameras can. Consumers seem to need more stimuluses [stimuli] than ever before, which is why Apple's portable iPad has enjoyed such enormous success.

3. The heros [heroes] of the younger generation are people such as Mark Zuckerberg and Bill Gates, the founders of tech giants Facebook and Microsoft. In fact, the paparazzis [paparazzi] follow those men. When people read about the lifes [lives] of entrepreneurs such as Gates, they dream about owning million-dollars [dollar] homes, too.

EXERCISE 3 DETERMINERS

PART A

Fill in the blanks with *much* or *many*.

1. These days, people provide too ___much___ information to others. There have been ___many___ instances in which someone has been embarrassed by a cellphone video. For example, there are ___many___ stories on the Internet about the infamous "Dog Poop Girl" from Korea. She received too ___much___ publicity for a silly mistake. While riding on a Seoul subway, she irritated ___many___ fellow passengers because she refused to pick up her dog's poop. Another passenger didn't waste ___much___ time before he put photos of her online. She received so ___much___ negative attention that she dropped out of university.

PART B

Fill in the blanks with *little* or *few*.

2. The Internet has provided a new way for people to anonymously enforce social norms. In the past, there were only a ___few___ ways to get shamed publicly for violating a social norm. Very ___few___ people used to carry cameras, and there were very ___few___ public security cameras. In the past, other passengers in the Dog Poop Girl's subway car might have gotten a ___little___ uncomfortable, but they couldn't have shamed her in front of the whole world. Before smart phones and the Internet, there was very ___little___ information available about people such as the Dog Poop Girl. A ___few___ local newspapers and magazines might have carried the story, but people elsewhere would have paid very ___little___ attention to the incident.

EXERCISE 4 *THIS, THAT, THESE,* OR *THOSE*

PART A

Underline and correct five errors involving *this*, *that*, *these*, or *those*. To review the rules for these determiners, see page 78.

EXAMPLE: These
<u>This</u> shoes that I'm wearing are too tight.

1. Do you see <u>this</u> (that) shoe store across the street? Last year, something terrible happened to it. In September, football fans were angry when our local team

lost. At this time, I was in my apartment watching television. I heard people shouting, so I looked outside. I saw a mob of fans walking up our street. Some of these people were throwing stones. Then I heard a crashing sound. Rioters smashed the windows of the store and stole all of the shoes. The store owner felt angry about what had happened and said, "Why did that people destroy my window? This days, my insurance costs are too high, and I can't stay here anymore."

PART B

For each group of words in parentheses below, circle the best choice to complete the sentence.

EXAMPLE: I've been feeling quite lonely (these / those) days.

2. In the early 1800s, public shaming in Canada was common. Some (persons / people / peoples) were flogged in public for committing criminal acts. In (this / that / these / those) days, even branding was permitted as a form of punishment! At (this / that / these / those) time, the goal of the justice system was to punish rather than rehabilitate criminals. Now, (this / that / these / those) days, such brutal forms of punishment no longer exist in Canada.

PRONOUN AGREEMENT

A pronoun must agree with its **antecedent**, which is the word that the pronoun refers to.

The Milgram experiment (antecedent) had **its** (pronoun) debut in 1961.

Subject Pronoun or Object Pronoun?

When a pronoun is paired with another noun, the correct choice of pronoun isn't always obvious. A simple way to determine the correct pronoun is to say the sentence with just that pronoun.

The professor asked Martin and (**I** or **me**) to present our topic.

Possible choices: The professor asked **I**. / The professor asked **me**.
Correct answer: The professor asked Martin and **me** to present our topic.

Pronouns in Comparisons

When a pronoun follows a comparison that uses *than* or *as*, ensure that you use the correct pronoun. To verify that your pronoun is correct, complete the thought.

I like psychology better than (**he** or **him**).

Complete the thought: I like psychology better than **he** (likes psychology).

TIP

Commonly Confused Pronouns

The following pronoun pairs sound alike but have different meanings.

Its is a possessive adjective. ***It's*** is the contraction of "it is."

The store has **its** annual sale. **It's** a great time to shop.

Your is a possessive adjective. ***You're*** is the contraction of "you are."

You're late, but **your** excuse is original.

Their is a possessive adjective. ***There*** indicates that something exists.

There are many people who dislike **their** jobs.

Hal Niedzviecki

To choose the correct pronouns in Exercise 5, remind students to complete the thought. For example, in number three, the complete third sentence would be: "It seemed like the producers were more excited about the project than he and his wife (were)."

EXERCISE 5 **MIXED PRONOUNS**

Underline the appropriate words in parentheses.

EXAMPLE: My friend and (I / me) watched the video.

1. Hal Niedzviecki decided to embark on an interesting experiment. He allowed cameras to film (him / himself) twenty-four hours a day for the documentary *Peep Culture*. Filmmakers Sally Blake and Jeannette Loakman installed (theirselves / themselves / themself) in a studio near Niedzviecki's home, and they edited the footage that they received. The documentary was (there / their / theirs) idea, even though Niedzviecki was the subject. (He / Him) and his wife agreed to the project.
2. (There / Their / They) were many reasons Niedzviecki chose to make the documentary. (Her / His) book *The Peep Diaries* had made (her / him / himself) a minor celebrity after (she / it / he) was selected by Oprah Winfrey's magazine *O* as a must-read book in 2009. Before agreeing to do the documentary, Niedzviecki did not have a Facebook account, Twitter account, or blog. After agreeing to the documentary, (he / him) decided to get all three.
3. At first, Niedzviecki felt shy in front of the camera. Neither (he / him) nor his wife loved to be filmed constantly. It seemed like the producers were more excited about the project than (he / him) and his wife. Eventually, Hal became comfortable, and he started to consider what his viewers thought about (he / him). His wife said, "Hal was in front of the camera more than (I / me). I didn't let the filmmakers come upstairs."
4. Niedzviecki thinks that the downside of "peep" culture is that everybody wants to be famous. (Its / It's) detrimental to our social development. Think of all the aspects of (your / you're) life that are affected by peep culture.

PRONOUNS: SPECIAL RULES

Pronouns after *And, Or,* and *Nor*

When two or more nouns are joined by *and*, use a plural pronoun to refer to them.

Milgram **and** Zimbardo published **their** results.

When the nouns are joined by *or* or *nor*, the pronoun form is the same as the form of the noun that is nearest to it.

singular form
Does either Milgram **or** Zimbardo have regrets about **his** experiment?

plural form
Neither the man **nor** the women removed **their** glasses.

Pronouns after *One of the / Each of the*

In a sentence containing the expression *one of the* or *each of the*, the subject is the indefinite pronoun *one* or *each*. You must use a singular pronoun to refer to the subject.

One of the women spoke with **her** lawyer.

Indefinite Pronouns

When the antecedent is a singular indefinite pronoun such as *everybody*, *something*, or *nobody*, use a singular pronoun to refer to it.

At the men's club, nobody had a chance to voice **his** objection to the new rule.

If the gender of the subject is unknown, or if the subjects include both genders, use both the male and female pronouns. If the sentence then appears awkward, simply change the subject to the plural form.

Incorrect: Everybody must submit **their** answers to the professor.
Solution: Everybody must submit **his or her** answers to the professor.
Better solution: The students must submit **their** answers to the professor.

Students may find examples in the media of plural pronouns referring to singular antecedents such as *everybody*. Occasionally, the incorrect pronoun is used because of the context. For example, the following sentence is technically incorrect, yet *they* cannot be substituted: "Nobody called, did they?"

You might point out that rules of the English language can change over time; for example, the pronoun *thou* has all but disappeared. Eventually, perhaps words such as *everybody* will be considered plural.

Some of the sentences in Exercise 6 are tricky. You might suggest that students underline the antecedents in each sentence.

EXERCISE 6 WRITING PRONOUNS

Write the appropriate pronoun or possessive adjective in the blanks.

EXAMPLE: He conducted the experiment in ___his___ laboratory.

1. Solomon Asch was a social scientist. One of his most well-known experiments had _____its_____ debut in 1951. In a small room, he conducted _____his_____ classic study about conformity. He gathered a group, and _____it_____ consisted of about ten participants. The people believed that _____they_____ were in an experiment to test _____their_____ visual judgment. Each person was led into a room filled with other people. What the participants didn't realize was that everybody else in the room had _____his or her_____ role to play. In fact, all the participants were actors except for the subject. Everyone was shown a line, and then _____he or she_____ had to state which line from among a new set was similar to the first line. The correct answer, B, would be obvious to the average person if _____he or she_____ looked carefully.

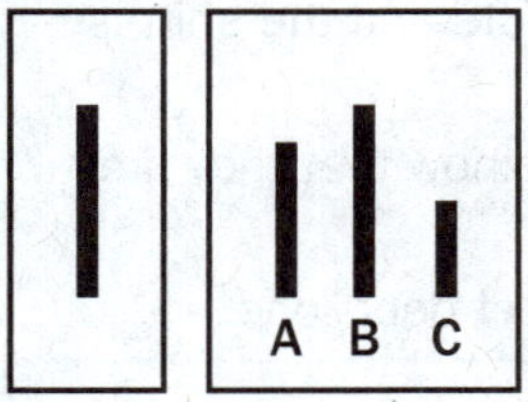

→

2. Everyone working for Asch knew that ___he or she___ must give the wrong answer. Asch wanted to know if the unsuspecting subject would give the same incorrect answer as the others in the group. In the first test, a male subject listened to the other participants, and then made sure ___his___ answer would match those of the others in the room. Neither the first nor the second male subject answered correctly, even though ___he___ clearly knew what the correct answer was. In fact, over one-third of the subjects answered the question incorrectly because ___they___ wanted to conform to the group. Those who disagreed with the others in the group expressed extreme discomfort. ___They___ fidgeted, looked at ___their___ hands, and appeared nervous.

AVOID VAGUE PRONOUNS

When you use pronouns, the antecedent (the person or object that the pronoun refers to) should be clear to the reader. Avoid using confusing pronouns such as *it* and *they* that have no clear antecedent.

Vague: They say that most people are conformists. (Who are *they*?)
Clearer: **Psychologists** say that most people are conformists.
Vague: It said in a magazine that some ads manipulate children. (Who or what is *it*?)
Clearer: **A magazine writer** claimed that some ads manipulate children.

In an essay that contains a repeated pronoun, such as *he* or *they*, make sure that the antecedents are clear.

Many teens try to be rebellious. Often, their actions worry their parents. They [**The parents**] surely want them to be happy and healthy. Sometimes discussions aren't enough for them [**the teens**]. They lose their [**their parents'**] trust and then they don't know what to do.

Read the sentences about teens aloud, without saying the corrections, to demonstrate how the references to *they* are unclear.

TIP

Consistent Point of View

When you write a paragraph or essay, make sure that your pronouns are consistent. Don't shift pronouns unless you're adding a supporting anecdote and the shift is logical.

Everyone needs to feel loved and respected. When people know that they are important to somebody else, it helps ~~you~~ [**them**] to make the correct decisions.

EXERCISE 7 IDENTIFYING PRONOUN ERRORS

Underline and correct twelve errors involving pronoun usage.

EXAMPLE: Our guests forgot to bring <u>there</u> [their] smart phones.

1. In this high-tech age, some new psychological problems have come to light. If someone sends you a text message, do you respond to <u>them</u> [him or her] immediately? Do you constantly write on <u>you're</u> [your] Facebook wall? <u>They</u> [Experts] say that compulsive texting may be a sign of a psychological addiction. It's also known that frequent Internet users experience cravings and withdrawal. If <u>your</u> [you're] online for several hours each day, you might have a problem.

Answers may vary.

2. Last summer, my partner Victor and <u>me</u> [I] tried to avoid online social networks for one month. It was difficult for Victor and <u>I</u> [me]. Our friends continued to post on <u>there</u> [their] Facebook pages, but we resisted. My cousins Angela and Kaylee also tried to stop using social media. However, they were less successful than Victor and <u>me</u> [I]. They both posted comments on <u>there</u> [their] Facebook walls. In the end, we enjoyed the experience and concluded that people feel better when <u>you're</u> [they're] not tied to a schedule of checking Facebook and Twitter every few hours. Giving up some online activities was a great experience for Victor and <u>I</u> [me]. We lived real lives instead of online lives. Facebook has <u>it's</u> [its] benefits, but real life is even better.

UNIT Review

Complete the following exercises. If you don't know an answer, go back and review the appropriate section.

1. Underline the six noncount nouns in the list below. Remember that a noncount noun doesn't have a plural form.

<u>advice</u>	animal	assignment	children	dollar	<u>equipment</u>
<u>homework</u>	<u>information</u>	<u>music</u>	person	<u>research</u>	suitcase

2. Underline and correct the errors in the following sentences. Then write a rule about each error.

   a) He made a two-<u>millions</u>-dollar investment. million

   Rule: Adjectives are never plural.

→

b) In 2009, I had a good year because this year, I earned a lot of money. that

Rule: Use *that* to refer to something that is distant in time or space.

c) I needed more informations about the product. information

Rule: *Information* is a noncount noun.

d) There were less customers at the bank today than there were yesterday. fewer

Rule: Use *fewer* with count nouns.

3. For each sentence, underline the correct pronoun in parentheses.

a) You should lock (you're / your) car doors unless (it's / its) a very old vehicle.

b) Neither Jake nor his brother ate (his / their) supper.

c) Please don't try to sell that product to Tim and (I / me).

d) Everyone puts useless items in at least one of (their / his or her) kitchen drawers.

e) You earn more money than Bruno or (I / me).

COMPANION WEB+ Need more practice? Visit the Companion Website and try additional grammar exercises.

Final Review

PART A

Underline the appropriate words in parentheses.

1. In the 1980s, people had a lot of privacy. In (this / these / those) years, nobody carried cellphones. If someone committed an illegal action, (they / he or she) could get away with it. But now, everything has changed. These days, many people's transgressions end up on YouTube. A new trend known as "Internet vigilantism" is sweeping cyberspace. (Much / Many) ordinary citizens have been affected by it.

2. For example, I was with some friends at a Stanley Cup hockey game. After the game, someone asked my friend and (I / me) to go to a club. On our way there, we entered a riot zone where people were breaking windows and robbing stores. We saw an acquaintance steal a few (piece / pieces) of (electronic / electronics) (equipment / equipments). Another friend was carrying two-(hundred /hundreds)-

You can use the Final Review as a test. There are twenty answers in Part A and five answers in Part B for a total of twenty-five points. You can also find additional practice exercises and testing material on the Companion Website.

(dollar / dollars) jeans. I was surprised by the stealing, but my friend was more shocked than (I / me). We wanted to leave the riot zone right away, but neither the bus nor the subway had (their / there / its / it's) schedule posted where we could easily see it. Finally, someone offered my friend and (I / me) a lift.

3. Later, we were very glad that we hadn't engaged in the looting. A Facebook group targeted rioters, and (their / its / it's) purpose was to name and shame them. In the past, police would have had very (few / little) (information / informations) about the rioters. But a few hours after the hockey riot, almost everybody had (their / his or her / they're) picture on Facebook. (Thousand / Thousands) of (persons / people / peoples) called the police with the names of rioters. One rioter was so depressed after her name appeared in the news, she underwent a three-(week / weeks) stay in a hospital. Police have some (advice / advices) for people who want to riot: think twice before acting.

PART B

Underline and correct five errors involving nouns, pronouns, or determiners.

4. Over the years, many riots have been described in the medias (media). In Andrew Potter's text, "Rioting Is Fun," he argues that everyone would riot if they (he or she) could. According to Potter, most persons (people) would enjoy stealing and looting. During a hockey riot, for instance, spectators might have very few (little) control over their own responses. I disagree with Potter. If someone asked my friends and I (me) to participate in a riot, we would refuse.

SPEAKING AND WRITING

Once students have finished the writing exercise, ask them to exchange their writing with their teammates and to peer edit for proper use of nouns, determiners, and pronouns, including the correct use of singular and plural forms.

Material Possessions

Think about the most significant items that you own. Consider large items such as a car or smaller items such as a piece of jewellery, a photo, or an electronic item. In a team with two other people, share information about your belongings. Explain why you value certain items. Then, on a piece of paper, write a paragraph about your two partners and their items. List the material objects each person values, and describe their reasons for valuing those objects.

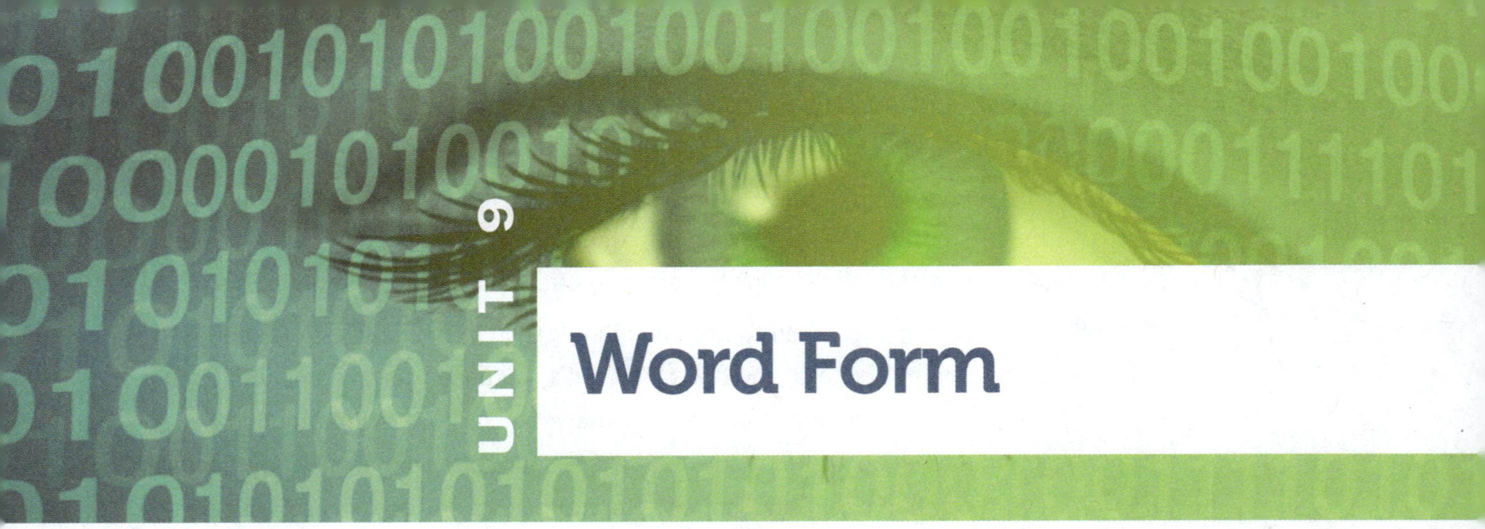

UNIT 9 Word Form

Use the Preview activity to introduce the passive voice. You could ask students to work on the activity in teams and make the activity a competition: students write their sentences on the board, and the team with the most correct answers wins.

Preview

PASSIVE VOICE CHALLENGE

Verbs can be either **active** or **passive**. When a verb is passive, the subject does not perform an action. Instead, the subject is affected by the action.

Active: Chandra **made** the coffee.
Passive: The coffee **was made** by Chandra.

Answers may vary.

With a partner, rewrite the following sentences so that they are in the passive voice, but keep verb tenses consistent. Note that the "by *subject*" phrase is not always needed.

EXAMPLE: Active: Workers plant corn in the spring.
Passive: Corn is planted in the spring (by workers).

1. Brad is using the iPad. The iPad is being used by Brad.
2. Korean workers build cars. The cars are built in Korea (by workers).
3. A stranger stole the car. The car was stolen (by a stranger).
4. I have made my choice. My choice has been made.
5. She will print the document. The document will be printed (by her).
6. We can help the homeless. The homeless can be helped (by us).
7. Mr. Lee had donated money. Money had been donated (by Mr. Lee).
8. We should have sold the house. The house should have been sold.

Passive Voice: Forms and Usage

For the **passive voice**, use the verb *be* + the past participle. It is preferable to use the **active voice**—except when emphasizing an action, versus the doer of the action. Use the passive voice sparingly.

Kurt **wrote** that story in 1961.

This is active because the subject (Kurt) performed the action.

That story **was written** in 1961.

This is passive because the subject (the story) was affected by the action; the subject didn't perform the action.

ACTIVE AND PASSIVE FORMS

VERB TENSE OR MODAL	ACTIVE (The subject is acting.)	PASSIVE (The subject is affected by the action.) *be* + past participle
simple present	Max teaches spies.	Spies **are taught** by Max.
present progressive	is teaching	**are being taught**
simple past	taught	**were taught**
present perfect	has taught	**have been taught**
past perfect	had taught	**had been taught**
future	will teach	**will be taught**
can	can teach	**can be taught**
could	could teach	**could be taught**
should	should teach	**should be taught**
would	would teach	**would be taught**
must	must teach	**must be taught**
should (past form)	should have taught	**should have been taught**

To Be

Use the past participle after *to be*.

Children need **to be loved**.

Gerunds and Infinitives: Forms and Usage

GERUNDS AS SUBJECTS

Usually, the subject of a sentence is a noun. A gerund is an "ing" verb that functions as a noun.

Exercising is important for the health.

GERUNDS AND INFINITIVES

When a verb appears after another verb, use the infinitive form for the second verb most of the time. The infinitive consists of *to* + the base form of the verb. But note that some verbs should be followed by gerunds.

Infinitive: We **need to leave**.
Gerund: Ryan **enjoys singing**.

Some Common Verbs Followed by Gerunds

acknowledge	consider	finish	miss	regret
admit	delay	involve	postpone	resent
adore	deny	justify	practise	resist
appreciate	detest	keep	quit	risk
avoid	discuss	loathe	recall	
can't help	dislike	mention	recollect	
can't stand	enjoy	mind	recommend	

Some Common Verbs Followed by Infinitives

afford	consent	hope	plan	swear
agree	decide	learn	prepare	threaten
appear	demand	manage	pretend	volunteer
arrange	deserve	mean	promise	want
ask	expect	need	refuse	wish
claim	fail	offer	seem	would like
compete	hesitate			

Some Common Verbs Followed by Gerunds or Infinitives

Some common verbs can be followed by either gerunds or infinitives. Both forms have the same meaning.

begin continue like love start

Gerund: He **continued** lying. **Infinitive:** He **continued** to lie.

Practice

EXERCISE 1 **IDENTIFYING ACTIVE OR PASSIVE VERBS**

Underline the appropriate verb form. Then indicate whether each answer is a passive verb or an active verb by writing either *P* or *A* in the blank.

EXAMPLE: Many soldiers (have disciplined / have been disciplined) __P__ for disobeying an order.

1. During times of war, armies (have sent / have been sent) __A__ soldiers on very dangerous missions. A soldier (can disobey / can be disobeyed) __A__ an order only if he or she (asked / is asked) __P__ to commit an illegal act. Even if soldiers (send / are sent) __P__ on missions they are unlikely to survive, they still have to obey. If an order (doesn't obey / isn't obeyed) __P__, the offending soldier (may arrest / may be arrested) __P__.

2. There are many instances in which the "I was obeying orders" defence (has used / has been used) __P__. For instance, in 1968, during the Vietnam War, American soldier Lieutenant William Calley (killed / was killed) __A__ more than one hundred civilians. Later, he claimed that he (had ordered / had been ordered) __P__ to kill "the enemy" by his superior officer. Military courts (oblige / are obliged) __P__ to press criminal charges against soldiers who carry out unlawful orders. Calley (sentenced / was sentenced) __P__ to life in prison. However, his prison sentence (reduced / was reduced) __P__ by President Richard Nixon in 1970.

EXERCISE 2 ACTIVE AND PASSIVE VERBS

PART A

Rewrite the following sentences so that they're in the passive voice: Change the verbs to the passive form. Don't alter verb tenses. Note that you don't always have to include the "by *subject*" phrase.

EXAMPLE: The supervisor *spies* on the workers.
The workers are spied on (by the supervisor).

1. Sometimes employers *place* spy cameras in the workplace.

   Sometimes spy cameras are placed in the workplace (by employers).

2. Last year, Mr. Roy *installed* three surveillance cameras.

   Last year, three surveillance cameras were installed (by Mr. Roy).

3. The video cameras *filmed* some sleeping workers.

   Some sleeping workers were filmed (by the video cameras).

4. As a result, the boss *has fired* three technicians.

   As a result, three technicians have been fired (by the boss).

PART B

Rewrite the following sentences so that they're in the active voice. Change the verbs to the active form. Don't alter verb tenses.

EXAMPLE: The workers *are spied* on by the bosses.
The bosses spy on the workers.

5. For months, Ben's privacy *has been violated* by the cameras.

   For months, the cameras have violated Ben's privacy.

6. Last week, a complaint *was made* to the police by Ben.

   Last week, Ben made a complaint to the police.

7. The case *will be investigated* by the union.

   The union will investigate the case.

8. Complaints about privacy *are often ignored* by companies.

   Companies often ignore complaints about privacy.

THE BASE FORM VERSUS THE PAST PARTICIPLE

Use the past participle (e.g., *moved*, *broken*, *seen*)

- of passive verbs and verbs that follow *to be*;

  The study was **completed** in 2012. It needs to be **published**.

- of verbs that follow *have*, *has*, or *had* in the perfect tenses.

  I have **read** many reports. The professor has **written** many books.

→

Use the base form (e.g., *go, eat, talk*)

- of verbs that follow the single word *to* in infinitive forms;

  She wanted to **move** to a suburb.

- of verbs that follow *do*, *does*, or *did* in question and negative forms.

  Did the participants **complete** the questionnaire?

TIP

Verb Form

Sometimes *be* is suggested but not written.
Sometimes the passive form can be written with just the final verb. Look at the following sentence. It has the passive form, so the past participle must be used.

The cost of wheat, **grown** in Albert, has risen.

missing words: *which* ***is***

Never write *to don't*.
When you use a negative infinitive, just put *not* before the infinitive.

The hacker decided ~~to don't~~ **not to** steal credit card information.

EXERCISE 3 **IDENTIFYING WORD-FORM ERRORS**

Underline and correct ten word-form errors.

EXAMPLE: Milgram's experiment is include [included] in most psychology textbooks.

1. In 1961, Stanley Milgram wanted to understood [understand] why ordinary Germans massacred innocent Jewish civilians during World War II. He created an interesting experiment. In 1974, his article, "The Perils of Obedience," was publish [published]. Since then, information about Milgram's study has appear [appeared] in most psychology textbooks.

2. Milgram's experiment showed how far people would go to obeyed [obey] authority figures. Each participant in the experiment was ask [asked] to administer electric shocks to another person. The subjects didn't realized [realize] that the other person was an actor. A few participants decided to don't [not to] give more shocks as soon as they heard the other

person scream. However, most of them administered the highest voltages even when the other person screamed in pain.

3. Milgram's experiment, study [studied] by students around the world, demonstrates that people will harm others if they are under orders to do so. The experiment showed how people are influence [influenced] by those in positions of authority. Many good people sometimes choose to don't [not to] listen to their own conscience.

TIP

Considered

Never write "considerated." It is not a word!

Milgram's study **considered** is ~~considerated~~ a classic.

CHOOSING *–ING* OR *–ED*

Some adjectives look like verbs because they end in *–ing* or *–ed*.

- When an adjective ends in *–ing*, it describes a quality of a person or thing.

  The **interesting** speaker described his experiences in Afghanistan.

- When an adjective ends in *–ed*, it describes a person or animal's expression or feeling.

  The **interested** audience listened carefully.

EXERCISE 4 WORDS ENDING IN *–ING* OR *–ED*

Underline the correct word in each set of parentheses.

1. In the past, the Central Intelligence Agency (CIA) was a (respecting / respected) institution, and its work was (considering / considerated / considered) important for the security of the United States. But in the early 1950s, the agency made a (surprising / surprised) decision. It hired McGill psychologist Dr. Ewen Cameron to do mind-control experiments on (unsuspecting / unsuspected) patients. Dr. Cameron was well-(compensating / compensated) for his work.

2. During the 1950s and 1960s, many patients arrived at Montreal's Allan Memorial Institute who had been (considering / considerated / considered) suicide. The (uninforming / uninformed) patients were (treating / treated) with the hallucinogenic drug LSD. Of course, they had (frightening / frightened) hallucinations. They were not (giving / given) accurate information about their treatment. Some deaths were (associating / associated) with the experiments.

3. Eventually, the nature of the experiments was (exposing / exposed) by investigative journalists. The public was (disturbing / disturbed) by the news. Many of Dr. Cameron's colleagues were upset about his (disappointing / disappointed) conduct. Cameron tried to rebuild his (damaged / damaging) reputation. Eventually, CIA Director William Colby apologized for the agency's (shocking / shocked) actions.

GERUNDS AFTER VERBS

When a verb appears after another verb, use the **infinitive form** for the second verb most of the time. But remember that sometimes the second verb should be a **gerund**, or "ing" verb.

Infinitive: He **wants** to leave. He **hopes** to graduate.
Gerund: He **enjoys** eating. She **finished** talking.

EXERCISE 5 GERUNDS AND INFINITIVES

Underline the appropriate verb form in parentheses. Remember that some verbs can be followed by both gerunds and infinitives (in these cases, underline both choices). If necessary, review the information about gerunds and infinitives on pages 91–92.

1. A person may plan (to betray / betraying) his or her country for many reasons. According to Christopher Andrew, co-author of *The Sword and the Shield*, the acronym MICE explains why a person might agree (to become / becoming) a traitor. MICE stands for "money, ideology, compromise, and ego."

2. According to Andrew, some people enjoy (to spend / spending) money so much that they will betray their countries for cash. They can't resist (to have / having) extra luxuries. Others hope (to have / having) some excitement in their lives. They don't mind (to commit / committing) dangerous acts.
3. Sometimes people decide (to believe / believing) in another country's ideology. They promise (to support / supporting) a country with different political views. Others can't avoid (to be / being) manipulated. In a court case, a man identified only as "Max B." mentioned (to become / becoming) a spy because someone was blackmailing him.
4. When Andrew finished (to write / writing) his book, he was surprised by the response. People really like (to read / reading) about spies.

STOP, *REMEMBER*, AND *USED TO*

Some verbs—such as *stop*, *remember*, and *used to*—can be followed by either an infinitive or a gerund, but the meaning of the sentence changes depending on the verb form you use.

FORM	MEANING	EXAMPLE
stop + infinitive	To stop an action in order to do something else.	He **stops** to buy gas every Sunday.
stop + gerund	To stop doing something permanently.	I **stopped** buying cigarettes five years ago.

→

FORM	MEANING	EXAMPLE
remember + infinitive	To remember to perform a task.	Please **remember to lock** the door.
remember + gerund	To have a memory about a past event.	I **remember meeting** him in 2005.
used to + infinitive	To express a past habit or situation.	Eva **used to live** alone.
used to + gerund	To be accustomed to something.	Eva is **used to living** alone.

EXERCISE 6 **GERUNDS AND INFINITIVES**

Underline the appropriate verb form in parentheses.

1. When William was a teenager, he (used to play / used to playing) poker every day. He remembers (to feel / feeling) nervous the first time he played. Like many adolescents, he wanted (to look / looking) cool. After a few months he enjoyed (to bet / betting) money on the games. He was soon (used to gamble / used to gambling). Almost daily, on his way home from school, he would stop (to gamble / gambling) at his friend's house.

2. About five years later, William subscribed to online casinos. He couldn't stop (to gamble / gambling). He was psychologically addicted, and he knew that he had (to do / doing) something. At one point, after he finished (to max out / maxing out) his credit card limits, he promised to quit (to play / playing) on casino sites. Still, whenever he was near the city's casinos, he would stop by a friend's house (borrowing / to borrow) some cash, and then he would gamble. His friend would say, "Please remember (to pay / paying) me back as soon as possible." William kept (betting / to bet) off and on for several more years.

3. On January 1, 2013, after his debts had reached critical levels, William realized that he needed (quitting / to quit). He decided (to take / taking) action right away. That night, he joined Gamblers Anonymous and stopped (to gamble / gambling). Nowadays, he (used to live / is used to living) without his habit. Sometimes he misses (to bet / betting), but then he remembers (to lose / losing) a lot of money and the respect of his friends and family. He hopes (to rebuild / rebuilding) his credit rating. He also plans (to grow / growing) up and behave like an adult. He wants to stop (to act / acting) immature.

PREPOSITIONS PLUS GERUNDS

Many sentences have the structure *verb + preposition + object*. Therefore, a gerund can be the object of a preposition.

She is tired of **working** nights.

Some Common Verbs + Prepositions Followed by Gerunds

accuse of	(be) enthusiastic about	insist on	(be) responsible for
be accustomed to	(be) excited about	(be) interested in	succeed in
apologize for	feel like	look forward to	think about
contribute to	(be) fond of	(be) nervous about	(be) tired of
discourage him from*	forgive me for*	prevent him from*	(be) worried about
dream of	(be) good at	prohibit from	

* Certain verbs are followed by a noun or pronoun plus a preposition.

EXERCISE 7 PREPOSITIONS AND GERUNDS

Fill in the blanks with the correct preposition + gerund of the verbs in parentheses.

EXAMPLE: Harry Harlow was enthusiastic (study) about studying the importance of love in a scientific context.

1. Before the 1960s, experts believed that mothers were excited (raise) about raising children and that breastfeeding contributed (create) to creating the maternal bond. They also thought that showing affection to children was sentimental and had no real role in child-rearing. Psychologist Harry Harlow was interested (test) in testing those ideas. He was accustomed (look) to looking at conventional ideas in original ways. Clearly, Harlow was very good (find) at finding interesting subjects for his experiments.

2. First, Harlow insisted (use) on using baby rhesus monkeys and separating them from their mothers. He prevented the baby monkeys (interact) from interacting with the outside world. Then he provided them with two fake mothers. One "mother" was made of soft cloth but had no food, while the other was made of coarse wire but had an attached bottle of milk. Harlow expected the "bottle mother" to get more attention from the babies, but, in fact, they were more interested (hug) in hugging the "cloth mother." When the cloth mother was removed from their cages for long periods, the baby monkeys would freeze up, scream, or cry.

3. Harlow was accused (be) of being cruel to the monkeys. He claimed that he never looked forward (hurt) to hurting the baby

monkeys, but, at the same time, he never apologized (deprive) for depriving them of a real mother and for stressing them intentionally to study their reactions. Ultimately, Harlow's study was responsible (change) for changing the perceptions of people in the scientific community. These days, everyone acknowledges the immense importance of a parent's caresses and affection. Eventually, Harlow became an alcoholic and was estranged from his own children. Nonetheless, his study succeeded (demonstrate) in demonstrating that babies and young children need affection to develop properly.

UNIT Review

Complete the following exercises. If you don't know an answer, go back and review the appropriate section.

1. For each of the following sentences, fill in the blank with the passive form of the verb *sell* in the appropriate tense.

EXAMPLE: Every day, many books are sold.

a) Last week, a new article was sold by the journalist.

b) Next year, a new book will be sold by Simmons Press.

c) Since 1990, over five hundred books have been sold by Simmons Press.

2. For each verb in parentheses, write either the gerund or infinitive form, as appropriate, in the space provided.

Amber Redmond enjoys (fly) flying. She wants (become) to become a pilot. She hopes (get) to get her pilots licence next March. Her mother said, "Stop (take) taking those lessons." However, Amber will finish (study) studying next month. She will become a pilot, and her mother can't prevent her from (do) doing it.

3. Underline and correct the error in each sentence.

a) Last year, Raoul developed a severe cough, so he stopped to smoke. Now he is a non-smoker. (stopped smoking)

b) Sophie tries to don't eat a lot of meat. (not to eat)

c) Raoul hates exercise, and he refuses walking in the woods. (refuses to walk)

d) Sophie avoids to be in the house while Raoul practises playing folk songs. (avoids being)

Need more practice? Visit the Companion Website and try additional grammar exercises.

Final Review

You can use the Final Review as a test. There are twenty answers in Part A and five in Part B for a total of twenty-five points. You can also find additional practice exercises and testing material on the Companion Website.

PART A

Underline the appropriate words in parentheses.

EXAMPLE: I would like (to know / knowing) more about the Omar Khadr case.

1. Do you remember (to hear / to hearing / hearing) about the Omar Khadr case? Although I usually avoid (to read / reading) about war, I am interested (to learning / learning / in learning) more about his situation. It is a complex case that has attracted a lot of controversy. Khadr was accused (to kill / killing / of killing) an American soldier in Afghanistan when he was only fifteen years old. In 2010, he was convicted of five charges.

2. Before Khadr's trial, many organizations, including UNICEF and the Canadian Bar Association, asked Canada (intercede / to intercede / to interceding) on Khadr's behalf because he was (considering / considerated / considered) a child at the time of his crimes. The Canadian government decided (to leave / leaving / for leaving) him in the United States. Some (informing / informed) members of the public were (surprising / surprised) by the Canadian government's (disturbed / disturbing) decision. Khadr's supporters did not succeed (to convincing / convincing / in convincing) government officials to change their minds. A 2004 documentary did not help Khadr's case. In the documentary, his mother and sister complained about Canada's liberalism and acknowledged (to feel / feeling / in feeling) pleased about the 9/11 attacks on the World Trade Center. At that point, some members of the public stopped (to care / caring) about Khadr.

3. What is your opinion about child war combatants? Some people argue that a fifteen-year-old boy can't help (to do / doing) what his father asks him to do. It's likely that no child enjoys (to live / living) in a war zone. Can a fifteen-year-old refuse (to follow / following) his parents' wishes? In Khadr's case, could he have stopped (to fight / fighting) and then left Afghanistan? Perhaps he was (used to live / used to living) amid violence and did not know what a normal childhood is. In the future, I hope (living / to live) in a less violent world. Perhaps, one day, people will believe that the murder of innocents can never be (justify / justified).

PART B

Make the following sentences passive. Don't alter verb tenses.

EXAMPLE: American soldiers arrested Khadr.
Khadr was arrested (by American soldiers).

4. In 2008, Michelle Shephard published a book about Khadr.
In 2008, a book about Khadr was published (by Michelle Shephard) ____________________.

5. Many stores sell the book.
The book is sold (by many stores) ____________________.

6. US interrogators may have tortured more prisoners.
More prisoners may have been tortured (by US interrogators) ____________________.

7. Eventually, authorities will release Khadr.
Eventually, Khadr will be released (by authorities) ____________________.

8. Khadr's case has influenced international law.
International law has been influenced (by Khadr's case) ____________________.

SPEAKING AND WRITING

Once students have finished the writing exercise, ask them to exchange their writing with another pair of students and then to peer edit for the proper use of active verbs and overall verb forms.

Edit a Letter

In the letter below, the writer overuses the passive voice. The letter would be clearer if the writer had used the active voice. With a partner, underline the passive verbs, and then rewrite the letter using the active voice.

Your e-mail has been received by us. You will be contacted by a support technician soon. Your problem will be solved by our technician. Additionally, your account will be credited and you will be provided with two months of free support. If you have any further questions, we can be contacted during working hours.

____

____

____

____

____

____

____

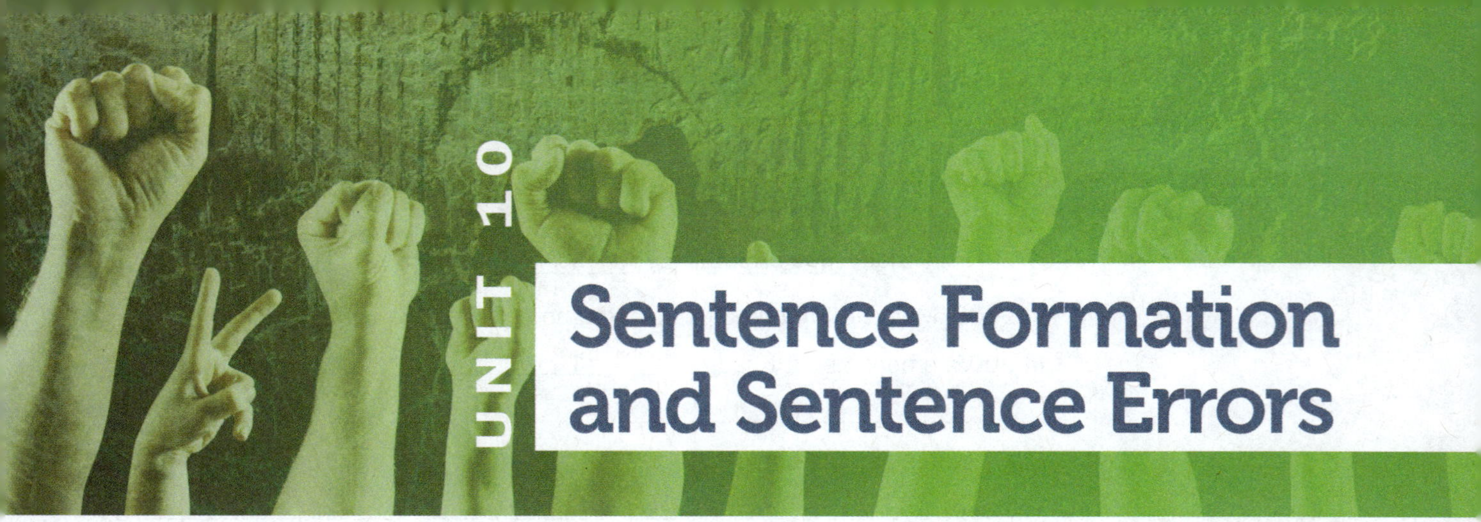

UNIT 10

Sentence Formation and Sentence Errors

You can use the Preview activity to review correct sentence structure.

Preview

IDENTIFY SENTENCE ERRORS

Write *C* next to sentences that are correct. Correct the errors in the other sentences.

1. Do you know what ~~is~~ the most important thing in life[^is]?
2. Friends and family are important~~, these~~ [. These] such connections help us navigate the world.
3. For example, dealing with a tragedy [^is difficult].
4. To get through a crisis, we must understand ourselves, accept our limits, and ~~maintaining~~ [maintain] an optimistic attitude.
5. The final step is to accept what we can't change. C
6. ~~Because we~~ [We] must be realistic when we face the future.

Sentences: Forms and Usage

To make your writing more interesting, you can combine sentences in a variety of ways. Review the following sentence types.

SIMPLE SENTENCES

A simple sentence has one **independent clause** (complete idea).

The fraud victims went to court.

COMPOUND SENTENCES

A compound sentence contains two or more independent clauses—or complete ideas—joined by a coordinating conjunction such as *and*, *but*, *or*, *nor*, and *yet*. You can also combine complete ideas with a semicolon. A third way to create a compound sentence is to join complete ideas with a semicolon and transitional expression such as *furthermore*, *however*, and *therefore*.

independent clause — independent clause

Some rioters broke the law, **and** they were arrested.

Some rioters broke the law; they were arrested.

Some rioters broke the law; **therefore,** they were arrested.

COMPLEX SENTENCES

A complex sentence contains at least one independent clause and one **dependent clause**. A dependent clause begins with a subordinator or a relative pronoun.

A **subordinator** joins the secondary idea to the main idea. Following is a list of common subordinators.

after	because	even though	when
although	before	unless	whereas

dependent clause — independent clause

Because they worry about the environment, they held a protest.

independent clause — dependent clause

Some students will complain **when** tuition fees increase.

A **relative pronoun** describes a noun or pronoun. The most common relative pronouns include the following:

that	which	who	whom	whomever	whose

independent clause — dependent clause

The rioter threw a rock **that** broke a window.

COMPOUND COMPLEX SENTENCES

To further add variety to your writing, you can also combine compound and complex sentences. The next example is a compound complex sentence.

complex sentence: Although Edward is shy, he is strong,

compound sentence: he is strong, and he is a very effective police officer.

Although Edward is shy, he is strong, and he is a very effective police officer.

COMMON SENTENCE ERRORS

FRAGMENTS

A fragment is an incomplete sentence. It is missing a subject, a verb, or a main clause. To correct a fragment, add the missing part or join it to another sentence. Review the following fragments and possible corrections.

	FRAGMENT	POSSIBLE CORRECTIONS
no subject	Have no children.	**Add a subject:** **Many couples** have no children.
no verb	First, the crime rate.	**Add a verb:** First, the crime rate **is dropping**.
no main clause	Because* he was hungry.	**Add a main clause:** **He stole food** because he was hungry.

* A subordinator such as *because* introduces a secondary idea. Make sure that your sentence also has a primary idea.

RUN-ON SENTENCES

A run-on sentence occurs when two complete ideas are joined incorrectly by a comma. Review the following run-on and some possible corrections.

RUN-ON SENTENCE	POSSIBLE CORRECTIONS
Jeremy left prison, he found a job.	**Add a coordinator:** Jeremy left prison**, and** he found a job.
	Add a subordinator: **After** Jeremy left prison, he found a job.
	Add a semicolon: Jeremy left prison**;** he found a job.
	Make two complete sentences: Jeremy left prison**. He** found a job.

Practice

SUBORDINATORS

Review some common subordinators

SUBORDINATORS	PURPOSE	EXAMPLE
as **because** **so that**	Indicate a reason or cause	He learned Karate **because** he wanted to be physically fit.
after **until** **before** **when**	Indicate a time	**After** he received his black belt, he returned to America.
as long as **if** **unless**	Indicate a condition	He will not fight with a stranger **unless** he feels threatened.
although **even though** **whereas**	Indicate a contrast	**Although** karate is difficult to learn, millions of people study it every year.

EXERCISE 1 **COORDINATORS AND SUBORDINATORS**

Underline the appropriate coordinating or subordinating conjunctions in parentheses.

EXAMPLE: Many quotes are attributed to famous people, (but / or / so) they are often wrong.

1. (When / Whereas / Although) Marie Antoinette moved to France, she had to adapt to a new culture. Many French citizens distrusted her (because / and / although) she was originally from Austria. Every morning, she would wear diamonds, (but / or / so) she would wear emeralds. She wanted to be good, (but / so / or) she sometimes visited poor neighbourhoods. At the same time, she lived in a palace (where / when / although) excessive luxury was the norm.

2. Marie Antoinette is one of the most famous queens in history, (or / so / but) she is not well known for a good reason. She is remembered for saying, "Let them eat cake." (Although / As long as / When) the phrase is popularly attributed to Marie Antoinette, some historians don't believe she said it. The phrase appeared in a book written (yet / when / so) she was only nine years old. The phrase also appeared in a book eight years before her birth, (so / but / or) she could not have been the first one to say it. These days, almost nobody knows King Louis XVI (unless / as long as / whereas) everyone has heard of Marie Antoinette.

RELATIVE CLAUSES

A relative clause is a dependent clause that is introduced by a relative pronoun. The following are some common relative pronouns and their purposes.

RELATIVE PRONOUNS	PURPOSE	EXAMPLE
that	Gives information about people or things	The project **that** I completed was easy.
which	Gives additional (non-essential) information about things	The movie, **which** has become a classic, stars Colin Farrell.
who **whom**	Give information about people (*Whom* is used in formal English to represent the object of a verb.)	The girl **who** lives next door is very nice. The man **who(m)** I met is married.
whose	Shows possession (*Whose* can replace *his*, *her*, *its*, or *their*.)	I met a man **whose** leg was broken.

TIP

Using *That* or *Which*

Both *that* and *which* refer to things, but *which* refers to non-essential ideas. In addition, *which* can imply that you are referring to the complete subject and not to just part of it. Compare the next two sentences.

The shirts **that** had stains provided DNA evidence.
(This sentence suggests that some shirts had no stains.)

The shirts, **which** had stains, provided DNA evidence.
(This sentence suggests that all of the shirts had stains.)

Here are two more examples to help students see the difference between *that* and *which*:

Bears **that** have white fur live in the Arctic.
Bears, **which** have white fur, live in the Arctic.

The second sentence incorrectly suggests that all bears have white fur.

TIP

Commas with *Which*

Generally use commas to set off *which* clauses.

> The rescue**,** which cost a lot**,** was well organized.

EXERCISE 2 RELATIVE CLAUSES

Fill in the blanks with *who*, *whom*, *that*, *which*, or *whose*. Note that in some cases, more than one answer is possible.

EXAMPLE: Last night, I read a story ____that____ was true.

1. Henry Molaison was a man ____who____ intrigued neurologists. In 1953, he underwent a procedure ____that____ was meant to cure his epilepsy. The new procedure, ____which____ was experimental, had an unintended side effect. After the surgery, Molaison, ____whose____ case has become well-known, was unable to form new memories.

2. By studying Molaison, psychologists and researchers learned certain things ____that____ they had never discovered before. One test, ____which____ was performed in the mid-1950s, involved giving Molaison meals. A researcher ____who(m)____ Molaison didn't recognize put a plate of food on the table in front of him. Molaison ate. A few minutes later, the researcher put another plate on the table and said, "Mealtime." Molaison, ____who____ had forgotten about his previous meal, happily ate another helping. Molaison, ____whose____ appetite was strong, felt full only after three meals.

3. A few years ago, I saw a movie ____that____ was about an amnesiac. The movie, ____which____ was excellent, was called *Memento*. The main character, ____whose____ name I don't remember, had a condition similar to Molaison's. *Memento*, ____which____ has become a cult classic, is a fascinating film about memory.

COMMONLY CONFUSED WORDS

Who's* and *Whose

Who's is the contracted form of *who is*.	**Who's** at the door?
Whose indicates possession and replaces *his*, *her*, *its*, and *their*.	**Whose** car is that?

Who* and *Whom

Who is the subject of a clause.	The detective **who** specializes in arson wrote a book.
Whom is the object of a clause.	The detective **whom** we met was helpful.

Than*, *Then*, and *That

Than is used to compare two things.	She is older **than** I am.
Then means "at a particular time."	He graduated and **then** found a job.
That introduces a clause.	The book **that** I read is very good.

TIP

Which

Ensure that you spell *which* correctly.

> The blog, ~~wich~~ which is new, discusses patriotism.

EXERCISE 3 **IDENTIFYING ERRORS**

Underline and correct fifteen usage and spelling errors involving *who*, *whom*, *which*, *than*, *then*, *that*, *who's*, and *whose*.

EXAMPLE: There are many people which [who] have contributed to revolutions

1. Wael Ghonim is a man which [who] played an important role in the Egyptian revolution of 2011. Ghonim supported slain protesters who's [whose] only crimes were opposing the regime of dictator Hosni Mubarak. Specifically, Ghonim's Facebook page, "We Are All Khaled Said," supported a young man whom [who] was killed while in police custody. Ghonim, a young computer entrepreneur working for Google, became a symbol for the young protesters, most of who [whom] were educated and tech-savvy. His web page helped organize the protests than [that] occurred nightly.

2. Ghonim's criticism of the Egyptian government, wich [which] angered President Mubarak, resulted in Ghonim's arrest. After he was released from jail, he appeared on a television show who [that] was seen by millions of Egyptians. During the interview, what [which] was shown on the Dream TV 2 network in Egypt, Ghonim talked about his cyber-activism. He said than [that] he was proud of the protesters in the streets. Than [Then], the next day, the number of protests escalated.

3. It was the public's anger than [that] eventually brought down the Mubarak government on February 11, 2011. Afterwards, everyone wondered, "Whose [Who's] going to lead the nation?" These days, Ghonim, whose [who's] respected and admired, doesn't feel like a hero. According to him, the people who's [whose] lives were lost are the true heroes of the revolution. The transition to democracy, which is not quite complete, has been difficult. Ultimately, the Egyptian revolution, who [which] was quite violent, has changed the political climate of the Middle East forever.

TRANSITIONAL EXPRESSIONS

Transitional expressions show the progression of ideas in an essay. You can place them at the beginning of sentences, and you can also use them to join two complete ideas.

Begin a sentence: However, the game was over.
Join complete ideas: Ray was losing the fight; however, he kept trying.

Some Common Transitional Expressions

Chronology:	first	second	finally	suddenly
Addition:	additionally	also	furthermore	moreover
Emphasis:	above all	clearly	of course	undoubtedly
Comparison:	however	in contrast	nevertheless	similarly
Conclusion:	in conclusion	in short	therefore	thus
Example:	for instance	in fact	for example	

Note: A more complete list of transitional words and expressions appears in Appendix 4, on page 178 of *Avenues 3: English Skills*.

TIP

Although or *However*

Do not confuse *although* and *however*. ***Although*** is a subordinator that means "even though." Don't put a comma after *although*. ***However*** is a transitional expression. Always put a comma after *however*.

> **Although** he broke the law, he didn't go to jail.
> He broke the law**; however,** he didn't go to jail.
> He broke the law. **However,** he didn't go to jail.

EXERCISE 4 SUBORDINATORS AND TRANSITIONAL EXPRESSIONS

Answers may vary.

Fill in the blanks with a subordinator or transitional expression from the list below. Use each choice once. The first one has been done for you as an example.

~~although~~	however	on the other hand	undoubtedly
eventually	meanwhile	subsequently	until
furthermore	nevertheless	thus	whereas

1. Dan Ariely, a professor of psychology at Duke University, has written about honesty in his book *The (Honest) Truth about Dishonesty*. ____Although____ most people like to believe that they are honest, they frequently fool themselves. ____Furthermore____, people from all classes and in all societies may be dishonest sometimes.

2. In April 2011, college student Dan Weiss was hired by the Kennedy Center for the Performing Arts in Washington, DC. His job was to take the stock inventory

at the centre's gift shop. Meanwhile, about three hundred well-intentioned volunteers worked at the shop. The shop sold $400,000 of merchandise. However, about $150,000 was disappearing each year. The gift shop had no cash registers, just a cash box that volunteers put the money into.

3. Weiss was determined to find the thief. Undoubtedly, the thief was one of the volunteers. He suspected a young man who brought the cash box to the bank each night. Weiss set up a sting operation, putting some marked bills into the box. Then, one night, Weiss and a detective waited patiently in a bush outside the bank until the shop closed. Later, when the young volunteer left the bank, they searched him. He had $60 of marked bills in his pocket. Subsequently, he was fired from his job. Nevertheless, the thefts continued. Thus, there had to be other thieves.

4. Eventually, Weiss discovered that hundreds of the volunteers were pilfering objects or money. He decided to put a cash register and an itemized logbook into the gift shop. Before, money disappeared every day whereas after the cash register was installed, no money disappeared. From this story, we can learn the following lesson. On the one hand, all types of people can be dishonest. On the other hand, people's bad behaviour can easily be modified.

EXERCISE 5 CHOOSING THE RIGHT WORD

Underline the appropriate word in parentheses.

EXAMPLE: I read a story (who / that) was sad.

1. I read a story about a man (who's / whose) life was very difficult. Mohamed Bouazizi was a Tunisian street vendor (who / who's / whose) wares were continually taken by the police. He lived in a city (who / where / what) ordinary citizens were continually harassed. On the morning of December 16, 2010, he borrowed about US$200 to buy produce (who / where / that) he would sell at the market. As usual, a police officer, (whom / whose / who's) Bouazizi recognized, appeared on the street. (However / Although) street-cart vendors didn't need permits, the officer asked to see one. Bouazizi did not have money to bribe the officer; (therefore / because / although), the officer took Bouazizi's electronic weighing scale and tossed his produce on the ground.

→

2. That afternoon, the twenty-seven-year-old man, (whose / who / whom) heart was racing, ran to the governor's office to complain. He asked for his weighing scale back; (although / however), he was ignored. In desperation, Bouazizi bought a can of gasoline from a gas station (who / that) was nearby. Then he set himself on fire.

3. Bouazizi's self-immolation was the catalyst (who / when / that) sent protesters into the streets. For weeks, they gathered in squares. (However / Although) the Tunisian president, Ben Ali, visited Bouazizi in the hospital, it didn't help the president's reputation. One month later, in January, Ben Ali fled the country, (who / what / which) was a wise choice. Today, he is a man (who's / whose / which) living a life of luxury in Saudi Arabia. In the meantime, Tunisia is a nation (who / that / who's) is building a democracy.

Draw attention to problems with embedded questions. You might put extra examples on the board. You could write questions such as "How old is he?" or "Why did he plead guilty?" and then ask students to change them into embedded questions by adding *Do you know* or *I wonder*.

CONSTRUCTING EMBEDDED QUESTIONS

It is possible to combine a question with a statement or to combine two questions. The result, an embedded question, is set within a larger sentence. Such embedded questions do not require the usual question word order, added auxiliaries, or, in some cases, even question marks. As you review the following examples, pay attention to word order.

Question	**Embedded Question**
Why do people commit crimes?	He asked why people commit crimes.
How should we proceed?	I wonder how we should proceed.

Use *if* or *whether* if there is no question word, or if the question word is not suitable in the embedded question.

Was he convicted?	Do you know **if** he was convicted?

TIP

Use the Correct Word Order

When you edit your writing, ensure that you have formed any embedded questions properly.

Dr. Alvarez wonders why ~~do~~ people commit crimes. I asked her what ~~did she think~~ **she thought** about the issue.

EXERCISE 6 CREATING EMBEDDED QUESTIONS

Complete the following embedded questions.

EXAMPLE: What does he want? I wonder what he wants.

1. How old is the suspect? Do you know how old the suspect is?
2. Why was she arrested? I wonder why she was arrested.
3. Does she have an alibi? Can you tell me if she has an alibi?
4. Where did the crime occur? I don't know where the crime occurred.
5. Should we watch the trial? I wonder if we should watch the trial.
6. What will the jury decide? We discussed what the jury will decide.

The president of Russia Vladimir Putin and former Egyptian president Hosni Mubarak

EXERCISE 7 IDENTIFYING EMBEDDED-QUESTION ERRORS

Underline and correct six errors involving embedded questions.

EXAMPLE: The writer explains how ~~can people~~ people can hold on to power for so long.

1. Around the world, citizens wonder why ~~are~~ so many nations are run by dictators and authoritarian regimes. They also question how ~~were~~ certain leaders were able to accumulate their wealth. For example, people want to know how ~~did~~ former Egyptian president Hosni Mubarak <u>become</u> became so wealthy.

2. To understand the former Egyptian president's wealth, people should consider why ~~was~~ Mubarak was admired and supported by the international political community during his reign. Around the world, democratic Western nations tend to support undemocratic regimes when it is good for international business. For example, if someone wonders how ~~could~~ Mubarak could have remained in power for eighteen years, he or she should evaluate the situation. About 4 percent of the world's oil supply must pass by boat through the Suez Canal in Egypt. Perhaps that explains why ~~did~~ Mubarak <u>ensure</u> ensured business went smoothly for the companies and nations that needed to use the canal. He established mutually beneficial friendships with international leaders.

IDENTIFYING FRAGMENTS AND RUN-ON SENTENCES

A sentence must have a subject and a verb, and it must express a complete idea.

A **fragment** is an incomplete sentence.

A **run-on sentence** occurs when two or more complete sentences are incorrectly connected. Note that you can't join two complete sentences with a comma. Also note that very long sentences are not necessarily run-ons.

Fragment: Although there was no evidence.

Run-on: The case went to court**,** the eyewitness was compelling.

Complete sentence: Although there was no evidence**,** the case went to court **because** the eyewitness was compelling.

TIP

Ask students to corrrect the sentences in the tip box.

Adding Examples

When you add an example to prove a point, be particularly careful that your new sentence is complete. The next fragments were taken from student essays.

For example, when they made the prisoners clean toilets in "The Stanford Prison Experiment."

Like Milgram's experiment when people obeyed an authoritarian figure.

Explain that long sentences aren't necessarily run-on sentences. A run-on sentence is punctuated incorrectly.

EXERCISE 8 FRAGMENTS AND RUN-ONS

For the following sentences, write *F* beside the ones that are fragments and *RO* beside the run-ons. Write *C* beside the sentences that are correct.

Manoubia Bouazizi, mother of Mohamed Bouazizi, posing with a poster of her late son

EXAMPLE: The streets were quiet. C

Because soldiers patrolled them. F

1. Because street vendor Mohamed Bouazizi lit himself on fire. F
2. He wanted to protest against the Tunisian government. C
3. Which sparked a cultural revolution. F
4. Riots erupted in the Middle East, cities burned. RO
5. Until the end of the 2011. F
6. Activists living under the repressive regime took a chance and decided to fight for change. C
7. The Tunisian government fell, nobody knew who would lead the nation. RO
8. For example, when the president resigned and fled the country. F
9. Social media played a role, students communicated using Facebook. RO

EXERCISE 9 IDENTIFYING SENTENCE ERRORS

Underline and correct ten sentence errors involving fragments and run-ons. Use a variety of correction methods. Note that there may be more than one way to correct the errors.

EXAMPLE: The case was over~~,~~; the defendant was innocent.

Answers may vary.

1. There are many debates about acceptable behaviour during political protests~~.~~ ~~Such~~ , such as the question of the legitimacy of violent action. Some activists believe in passive resistance~~,~~; others feel that aggressive force is sometimes necessary.

2. In 2010, some protestors at the G20 Toronto Summit committed acts of vandalism and looting, so police responded forcefully. It was considered the ~~The~~ largest mass-arrest in Canadian history. Since then, many activists have criticized police tactics~~.~~ ~~Which~~ , which included intimidation and even assault. However, others have supported the police~~, they~~. They want the vandals to be punished. Some of the G20 protestors received prison sentences~~. Including~~ , including Alex Hundert. He was arrested before the protests even started and was charged with conspiracy.

3. During Quebec's 2012 student strikes, most of the protesters were peaceful~~,~~; however, others were not. On May 10, 2012, smoke bombs were thrown into three subway stations~~. Causing~~ , causing chaos. Citizens were divided. Some supported the student protestors, but others criticized protestors' actions.

FAULTY PARALLEL STRUCTURE

Pairs or groups of items in a sentence should have a balanced grammatical structure within that sentence. Faulty parallel structure occurs when equivalent ideas are presented with different grammatical structures.

Not parallel: The detectives worked slowly and were careful.
Parallel adverbs: The detectives worked <u>slowly</u> and <u>carefully</u>.

Not parallel: They were people who were trained, who were professional, and having high standards.
Parallel clauses: They were people <u>who were trained</u>, <u>who were professional</u>, and <u>who had high standards</u>.

To identify faulty parallel structures in a sentence, look at the repeated grammatical units and then rewrite the unit that isn't parallel to the others.

EXERCISE 10 FAULTY PARALLEL STRUCTURE

Underline and correct the parallel structure error in each sentence. Write *C* beside the sentences that are correct.

EXAMPLE: I enjoy reading and to learn about psychology. learning

1. Aggressive behaviour can involve bodily contact such as biting, hitting, or to push. pushing
2. In fact, aggression can be physical or verbal. C
3. In the 1930s, some doctors, psychologists, and people who do research tried to identify the causes of aggressive behaviour. researchers
4. The scientists thought that their work was exciting and a challenge. challenging
5. In 1939, experimenters removed the temporal lobe from some monkeys that were friendly, active, and who had good health. healthy
6. After the surgeries, the monkeys showed no fear of snakes or humans. C
7. The doctors determined that the amygdala plays a role that is essential and has significance in fear responses. significant
8. The scientists hoped to learn more about how humans anticipate and dealing with fear. deal
9. In 1966, a man named Charles Whitman acted strangely and with violence. violently
10. Before his death in a shootout with police, Whitman wrote a note and was asking doctors to examine the state of his brain. asked
11. In fact, a later examination revealed the presence of a tumour next to his amygdala. C
12. Scientists believe that damage to the frontal lobe can contribute to behaviour that is controlling, sadistic, and causes people to abuse others. abusive

UNIT Review

Correct the errors in the following sentences. Then write a rule explaining each error. If you don't know an answer, go back and review the appropriate section.

1. First, the strangest experiment. (^ happened)

Rule: A sentence must have a subject and a verb, and it must express a complete idea.

2. A scientist conducted a test who was very successful. (who → that)

Rule: Do not use *who* to give information about things.

3. The test was about altruistic behaviour, it was fascinating. (^ and)

Rule: Do not join two complete ideas with just a comma.

4. I wondered why did they create the test. (did they create → they created)

Rule: Remove the auxiliary in embedded questions.

5. The researcher was helpful, friendly, and acted with generosity. (acted with generosity → generous)

Rule: A sentence should have parallel structure.

Companion Web+ Need more practice? Visit the Companion Website and try additional grammar exercises.

Final Review

PART A

You can use the Final Review as a test. There are five answers in each part, for a total of fifteen points. You can also find additional practice exercises and testing material on the Companion Website.

For each of the sentences, circle the letter of the answer that best fills in the blank. Note that *X* means "nothing."

1. Facebook and Twitter have a role in revolutions ___ activists use them to organize protests.

a) , b) ; (circled) c) : d) X

2. Malcolm Gladwell, ___ a well-known author, wrote an article ___ is about activism.

a) who's / that (circled) b) whose / that c) who's / than d) whom / that

3. Gladwell's views, ___ he discusses in *The New Yorker*, are original and interesting.

a) what b) wich c) who d) which (circled)

4. According to Gladwell, Facebook and Twitter are important ___, they do not have a significant impact on revolutions.

a) , however b) , although c) ; however (circled) d) ; although

5. Gladwell argues that social networking forms "weak ties" between people ___ it does not convince people to engage in protest.

a) because b) , so (circled) c) , which d) ; although

Answers will vary.

PART B

Underline and correct the errors in the following sentences.

EXAMPLE: I read an article <u>who</u> discusses violence. (that)

6. Americans can easily buy guns, ^ Canadians must get special permits. (but)

7. Last year, ^ many violent riots around the world. (there were)

8. Gladwell suggests <u>than</u> it's easier to be heard in a social network, but harder for each voice to make a difference. (that)

9. Sometimes protests become <u>violent. Because</u> opportunists take advantage of the chaos. (violent because)

10. Leaders who treat citizens fairly are more likely to be valued, respected, and <u>having support</u>. (supported)

You can ask students to remove this page and hand it in. Note that in the student books, pages are perforated.

PART C

Complete the following embedded questions. Remember to change the position of the verb in the sentence, if necessary.

EXAMPLE: Where are we? Do you know where we are?

11. What is the problem? Do you know what the problem is?

12. Why did they protest? I wonder why they protested.

13. Where are the police? Can you tell me where the police are?

14. How have the police reacted? I don't know how the police have reacted.

15. When should we discuss it? I wonder when we should discuss it.

SPEAKING AND WRITING

Letter to the Editor

Write a letter to the editor of a newspaper. Argue either that college tuition fees should increase or that they should not. Provide reasons for your opinion. Ensure that your letter has a variety of sentence types: simple, compound, and complex.

Ask students to exchange letters and peer edit for proper sentence structure.

UNIT 11

Punctuation and Capitalization

You can use the Preview activity to introduce punctuation and capitalization. Students can then complete the unit in class or for homework. Additional exercises appear on the Companion Website.

Preview

IDENTIFY PUNCTUATION ERRORS

Work with a partner. Identify and correct twenty errors in capitalization or punctuation.

Every Summer, my friend's meet in Halifax, Nova Scotia. Last august, on a saturday morning; we went for a drive along Shore road. We walked along Mahone bay, and we could see the Atlantic ocean. Suddenly, we heard screams for help. A twenty-two-year old woman was shouting. She was in the water and she could not get back to shore. Brad my brother in-law, had the presence of mind to do the following; take a rope from his car throw one end to the woman, and pull her to safety. Although, Brad had helped her, the woman was ungrateful. She was angry, "you should have jumped into the water to save me". Then she got into her car and drove away. We all agreed that she looked like a character from that television show called *Gossip girl*. Later, while we were driving to our hotel, Brad said; "I tried to do the right thing. She should'nt have been so ungrateful."

Punctuation: Forms and Usage

APOSTROPHES (')

Apostrophes in Contractions

Use an apostrophe to join a subject and a verb.

They**'re** popular. There**'s** a crowd outside the theatre.

Also use an apostrophe to join an auxiliary with *not*.

We ca**n't** see the show. There are**n't** any tickets left.

Apostrophes to Show Ownership

You can add an apostrophe followed by an –s (*'s*) to a noun to indicate possession.

Alicia is the child of Marco. She is Marco**'s** child.

If the noun is plural, put the apostrophe after the –s.

The boy**s'** clothes are in the washing machine.

If the noun has an irregular plural form, add –'s.

The men**'s** room is down the hall.

When two people have **joint ownership**, add the apostrophe to the second name.
When two people have **separate ownership**, add apostrophes to both names.

Joint ownership: Marian and **Jake's** gallery is successful.
Separate ownership: **Marian's** and **Jake's** studios are in different buildings.

COLONS (:)

Use a colon

- after a complete sentence that introduces a list, or after the words *the following*;

  The play has the following parts**:** crime, punishment, and redemption.
- after a complete sentence that introduces a quotation;

  Picasso's advice was clear**:** "Find your passion."
- to introduce an explanation or example;

  The drama ended with a lesson**:** enjoy life.
- to separate the hours and minutes in expressions of time.

  The movie begins at 7**:**30 and ends at 10**:**00.

COMMAS (,)

Use a comma

- after an introductory word, phrase, or idea;

  First**,** Mrs. Rice closed her store.
  A few minutes later**,** she emptied the safe.
- to separate three or more words in a series (you can put a comma before the word *and*);

  The building is tall**,** old**,** and decrepit.
- around an interrupting phrase that gives additional information about the subject;

  Jenna**,** a student at Montmorency College**,** went through a traffic light.
- with a quotation, after an introductory phrase.

  She said**,** "The light was green."

ELLIPSES (. . .)

Use the ellipsis to show that you have omitted unnecessary information from a quotation. When you type the three periods, leave a space before and after each period.

Seligman wrote, "The path is very clear. . . . We must work together."

HYPHENS (-)

Use a hyphen

- when you spell out a compound number between 21 and 99;

  twenty-five ninety-two seventy-seven
- after some prefixes, such as *ex-*, *mid-*, and *self-*;

  ex-husband mid-December self-assured
- with some compound nouns (note that *compound* means "more than one part");

  mother-in-law show-off sister-in-law
- when you use a compound adjective before a noun. The compound adjective must express a single thought.

  one-way street thirty-year-old woman well-known actor

PERIODS (.)

Use a period at the end of a complete sentence and with the following titles Ms., Mrs., Mr., and Dr. (Don't put a period after *Miss*.)

Mr. Fairhaven studied happiness and its effects on the brain.

QUOTATION MARKS (" ")

Use quotation marks around direct speech. Capitalize the first word in the quotation, and place end punctuation inside the closing quotation marks.

Oscar Wilde declared, "All art is useless."

Pradip asked, "What is the cost of that painting?"

SEMICOLONS (;)

Use a semicolon to join two independent and related clauses.

Gandhi was a pacifist; he believed in non-violence.

Capitalization: Forms and Usage

Always capitalize

- the pronoun *I* and the first word of every sentence;

  The man that I met is very nice.
- the days of the week, the months, and holidays;

  Friday June 8 Labour Day
- the names of specific places, such as buildings, streets, parks, public squares, lakes, rivers, cities, provinces, and countries;

  Evan Avenue Lake Erie Calgary, Alberta
- the names of languages, nationalities, tribes, races, and religions;

  Spanish Mohawk Protestant

- the titles of specific individuals;

  General **D**allaire | **P**rime **M**inister **L**ee | **M**rs. **P**eel
- the titles of specific school courses;

  Physics 201 | **E**nglish 101 | **B**eginner's **S**panish
- certain historical events, eras, and movements;

  World **W**ar II | **C**ubism | **G**roup of **S**even
- the important words in titles of literary or artistic works.

  ***O**n the **R**oad* | ***P**itch **P**erfect* | "**M**y **V**isit to **M**ontreal"

Practice

EXERCISE 1 APOSTROPHES

Write the possessive forms of the following phrases. To review apostrophe rules, see page 118.

EXAMPLE: the sister of the doctor — the doctor's sister

1. the brush of the artist — the artist's brush
2. the brushes of the artists — the artists' brushes
3. the pictures of Sandra — Sandra's pictures
4. the room of the child — the child's room
5. the rooms of the children — the children's rooms
6. the photo of Ross and Anna — Ross and Anna's photo
7. the car of Ross and the car of Anna — Ross's and Anna's cars

COMMON APOSTROPHE ERRORS

Don't use an apostrophe before the final *–s* of a verb or a plural noun.

Mr. Garcia ~~want's~~ **wants** to open several ~~gallery's~~ **galleries**.

In negative contractions, remember that the apostrophe replaces the *–o* of the word *not*. Therefore, the apostrophe comes **after** the letter *n*.

He ~~does'nt~~ **doesn't** understand the problem.

EXERCISE 2 IDENTIFYING APOSTROPHE ERRORS

Underline and correct fifteen errors involving apostrophes and possessive forms. Note that you may need to add, remove, or move apostrophes. You also may need to add a final *–s* to words.

EXAMPLE: What is an artists (artist's) motivation to create?

1. Many artist's (artists') paintings are unique. Have you ever heard of George Tooker? The American painters (painter's) work earned him the National Medal of Honor in 2007. Several of his painting's (paintings) have also appeared in New York galleries. Most art school's (schools') programs mention realist artists such as Tooker and Fernand Botero. In fact, Botero (Botero's) and Tooker's paintings hang in museums.

2. At first, George Tooker's parents did'nt (didn't) like his choice of career. They wanted him to focus on literature. But he disobeyed his parents (parents') wishes and worked as an artist. His paintings are part of the movement known as magic realism. What makes his work unique is it's (its) dark overtones. One of his most famous paintings is of a group of people trapped in a subway. Theyre (They're) gathered in a low-ceilinged subway car, incapable of escaping. Its (it's) a powerful and disturbing image.

3. Tooker's work was'nt (wasn't) popular during most of his life. In the recent past, most peoples' (people's) choice of favourite artist would not have been Tooker. However, now hes (he's) become a well-known realist painter and is known for making mundane situations seem ominous or threatening. His despondent view of the modern world has influenced contemporary artists. Youll (You'll) find his artwork in many art gallery's (galleries') collections.

SPECIAL COMMA RULES

Commas with *Who*, *Which*, and *That*

Review the comma rules in clauses beginning with *who*, *which*, or *that*.

- ***Which***

  Always use commas to set off clauses beginning with *which*.

  The brain, **which** is a complex organ, develops rapidly.

- ***That***

  Don't use commas to set off clauses beginning with *that*.

  The house **that** I grew up in was demolished last year.

→

To help students understand essential versus non-essential clauses, show them the next two sentences. *The man who torched the building was a dentist. The robber, who has two children, escaped from prison.* In the second example, the *who*-clause can be removed and the sentence still makes sense.

- ***Who***

  When a clause begins with *who*, you may or may not need a comma. If the clause contains **non-essential** information, put commas around it. If the clause is **essential** to the meaning of the sentence, it does not require commas.

  Essential: Many people **who** have brain injuries undergo subtle personality changes.
  (The underlined clause is essential to understand the meaning of the sentence.)

  Non-essential: Dr. Jay Geidd, **who** lives in Maryland, made an important discovery.
  (The underlined clause contains extra information, but if you removed the clause, the sentence would still have a clear meaning.)

Commas with Dependent Clauses

If a sentence begins with a dependent clause (a clause beginning with a subordinator such as *although* or *because*), place a comma after it. However, if the dependent clause appears in the middle of the sentence, no comma is necessary. Notice the difference in the next two sentences.

Comma: Because rents are so high, some young adults live with their parents.

No comma: Some adults live with their parents because rents are so high.

TIP

Comma Error

Don't separate the main subject and verb with a comma.

The researcher, was surprised with the results of the experiment.

EXERCISE 3 **EDITING FOR COMMAS**

Correct twelve comma errors by adding or removing commas, as appropriate.

EXAMPLE: Susanna Moodie, who was born in England, became one of Canada's most renowned authors.

1. In *Roughing It in the Bush*, Susanna Moodie wrote about living on a Canadian farm in the 1830s. Moodie, who enjoyed luxuries, did not enjoy life in the wild. At the same time, she was not a snob. People in different social classes, in Moodie's opinion, are separated only by the quality of their education.

Margaret Atwood

2. Moodie, who enjoyed writing, was asked to create a guide for immigrants from Britain. In her journals, she told British citizens what to expect when they arrived in Canada. Her anecdotes, which were filled with fascinating details, described the beauty and misery in Canada. She was also capable of humour. She said, "I have no wish for a second husband. I had enough of the first."

3. In the 1970s, Moodie's work increased in popularity because Margaret Atwood wrote poems about Moodie. Atwood, who was born more than a hundred years after Moodie, had written several bestselling novels. In Atwood's view, Moodie is one of the greatest writers in Canadian history.

HYPHENS

Remember to use a hyphen when a compound adjective appears before a noun. The compound adjective must express a single thought.

The department has a <u>two-way</u> mirror.
Detectives interviewed a <u>twenty-year-old</u> man.

Note: There is no hyphen if the compound adjective is after the noun. In addition, if the adjectives before a noun function independently, don't add a hyphen.

The man is twenty years old.	(The compound adjective is after the noun.)
Lange was a motivated, creative woman.	(The two adjectives function separately.)

TIP

Non-Hyphenated Compound Adjectives

Some compound adjectives never take a hyphen, even when they appear before a noun.

World Wide Web   health food store   real estate agent

EXERCISE 4 ADDING PUNCTUATION

Add twenty missing punctuation marks to the following paragraphs. When necessary, add a period, comma, colon, semicolon, hyphen, or apostrophe. You can review the information about punctuation on page 118.

EXAMPLE: The graphic novel, which is very old, is about teen heroes.

1. My brother in law loves manga illustrations. The name *manga* which means "whimsical drawings," defines a genre of animation. There are two popular forms of manga Shonen manga for men and Shojo manga for women. At the end of World War II Japanese manga comics were introduced to North America. After soldiers completed their tours of duty many of them brought the comics back to the US.

2. Early manga, which was mostly aimed at fifteen-year old boys focused on adventure stories. For example the comics dealt with robots, space travel and action heroes. When womens manga first appeared it was produced by men. However, in recent decades, most Shojo manga has been created by women. For example, Mrs Rumiko Takahashi is one of Japans wealthiest artists she has sold over 170 million comics. When the self assured artist first began her career, she worked with the following black pens, felt markers, and white paper.

➜

3. According to the magazine *Publishers Weekly*, the manga market in North America is now worth roughly $175 million. Many manga comics have content that may be sexually explicit, violent, or generally dark; thus, not everyone likes them. However, in comparison to other types of entertainment, manga is reasonably tame.

QUOTATIONS

Review the following details about how to punctuate quotations.

Opening Phrase or Sentence

In quotations, put a comma after the opening phrase. Put a colon after the opening sentence.

Comma: Pablo Picasso said, "Art is a lie that makes us realize the truth."
Colon: The critic was shocked: "What is Picasso doing?"

Interrupting Phrase

When a quotation is interrupted, place a comma after the first part of the quotation, and place another comma after the interrupting phrase.

"In the end," says dancer Martha Graham, "it all comes down to breathing."

Ending Phrase

When you place a phrase at the end of a quotation, end the quotation with a comma instead of a period.

"Great art picks up where nature ends," said Marc Chagall.

If your quotation ends with other punctuation, put it inside the quotation mark.

"Who is the greatest painter?" the student asked.
"That question cannot be answered!" the curator replied.

Integrated Quotation

If a quotation isn't a complete sentence, and you simply integrate it into your sentence, don't capitalize the first word of the quotation.

Dorothy Nixon calls herself a "terrible mother."

Quotations Inside Quotations

If one quotation is inside another quotation, then use single quotation marks (' ') around the inside quotation.

The young sailor was furious: "He was foaming with passion at the barbarous indifference manifested by the men in the boat. He said, 'If they had given me the oar in time, I could have saved him.'"

TIP

Page Numbers

Put the page number in parentheses. Place the final period after the parentheses. (Your teacher may ask you to indicate the paragraph number instead of the page number.)

Jan Wong wrote, "In July 1973, I prepared to leave China" **(122).**

EXERCISE 5 QUOTATIONS

In each sentence, the quotation is set in bold. Add capital letters, quotation marks, commas, or colons to the quotations, as necessary.

EXAMPLE: Professor Wayne Johnson asks, "**Where are the great female artists?**"

1. Famous music producer Rick Rubin says **right now, if you listen to pop, everything is in perfect pitch, perfect time, and perfect tune**
2. **Auto-Tune was originally created to fix pitch and tone problems in singers' voices** according to Anna Pulley.
3. **The Auto-Tune effect just worked for my voice** proclaimed rapper T-Pain.
4. **I know Auto-Tune better than anyone** said T-Pain **and even I'm just figuring out all the ways you can use it to change the mood of a record**
5. *Time* journalist Josh Tyrangiel says that technology **can transform a wavering performance into something technically flawless**
6. **It makes singers sound too perfect** says music lover Andrea Berezan **and perfect singing is boring**
7. Canadian recording artist Neko Case shows her contempt for Auto-Tune **when I hear Auto-Tune on somebody's voice, I don't take him seriously** (16)
8. **Too many pop stars also lip-synch in concert** declares Jay Segal.
9. Neil McCormack mentions an incident at a live show **I saw Madonna drop her microphone, and it didn't affect her performance** (28)
10. Music fan Chelsea Oberman says **When I pay $80 to see a live concert, and the singer lip-synchs, I sometimes shout use your voice**

CAPITALIZATION

Most capitalization rules apply to specific individuals, places, and school courses. If you make a general reference without giving a specific name, capitalization is unnecessary.

She lives on a nice street. It's called Kelvin Avenue.

EXERCISE 6 **CAPITALIZATION**

Add twenty missing capital letters to the following paragraphs. To review capitalization rules, see page 119.

L I W
EXAMPLE: Miku's best song is "love is war."

1. Hatsune Miku, with her turquoise pigtails and her sweet voice, has become a star in Asia. The article "Virtual Singer tops the charts" on *Web Japan* describes Miku: "She is no girl at all." Hatsune Miku is actually an artificial voice accompanied by a virtual avatar.

2. The british fashion magazine *Clash* featured Miku's virtual character on the cover of its fifty-ninth issue. The character has also appeared in the manga magazine *Comic rush*. Miku's voice is the result of a voice-synthesizing software program. It uses an audio library of samples from japanese voice actress Fujita Saki to create new, synthesized songs. In the article "Pixel perfect," Karley Sciortino describes the world of Miku. For under $200, aspiring songwriters buy the software program and then write songs for the virtual singer.

3. Crypton future media has made a lot of money from Miku. In 2007, Miku was the top-selling computer program in Japan. In april 2010, an updated version was released. In the newspaper *Los Angeles times*, journalist Tiffany Hsu wrote, "the virtual diva's albums have topped the Japanese charts." The character Miku also advertises products and has been a spokesperson for the Good Smile racing Company. Thousands of fans show up to Miku concerts. In august of 2009, at her first concert, Miku was projected to the audience as a giant 3-D hologram. There were Japanese, korean, and Chinese fans at the show. Some fans were buddhists and others were not. In july 2011, she performed at the Los Angeles convention Center, at 1201 South Figueroa street. Many students went to the show. Kylie Moreau, a student at Centennial high school, loved watching the hologram. Could Miku change the way music is produced?

PUNCTUATING TITLES

Place the title of a short work (such as a magazine article) in quotation marks. Italicize the title of a longer document (or underline titles in handwritten documents). Capitalize the first word and all major words in titles. It's not necessary to capitalize prepositions and articles.

	Short Work		Long Work
short story:	"The Lottery"	**book:**	*The Grapes of Wrath*
Web article:	"Music Artists Lose Out"	**website:**	*CBCNews*
newspaper article:	"Early Accomplishments"	**newspaper:**	*The Calgary Herald*
magazine article:	"The City's Hottest Ticket"	**magazine:**	*Rolling Stone*
essay:	"Hip-Hop Nation"	**textbook:**	*Common Culture*
TV episode:	"The Search Party"	**TV series:**	*Game of Thrones*
song:	"Mouths to Feed"	**CD:**	*Release Therapy*
poem:	"Howl"	**movie:**	*Man of Steel*

EXERCISE 7 **TITLE PUNCTUATION**

Add ten missing capital letters and punctuate seven titles. Add quotation marks where appropriate and underline titles that should normally be italicized.

In 2005, Terry Fallis hunted for a publisher for his book called The Best laid plans. His novel is about an ottawa politician who, despite his distaste for the political scene, is elected to canada's Parliament. When no publishers were interested, Fallis published his book by himself. Amazingly, his podcasts of book excerpts became popular. Then he won some literary awards. For example, he won the Canada Reads contest on february 9, 2011. His book beat Ami McKay's popular novel, The Birth house. In a newspaper interview with the Toronto star, in the column called afterword, Fallis said that a major publishing company would publish his novel for a mass audience. Since then, Fallis has published his second book, The High road. Grant Black, a reporter for The Globe and Mail, reviewed Fallis's second novel. In his article A Missed opportunity, Black wrote that the book "didn't deliver."

EXERCISE 8 IDENTIFYING PUNCTUATION ERRORS

Correct the errors involving punctuation or capitalization in the following sentences. Add underlines to titles that should be in italics. The number of errors in each sentence is indicated in brackets.

EXAMPLE: [1] Marcel Dzama, a well-known artist, does watercolour paintings.

1. [5] Last january, my brother was accepted into the Academy of fine arts on wellington street.

2. [6] He said "Did you see the article about creativity called "The left brain" in the Vancouver sun newspaper"?

3. [2] My father in law is a huge fan of Marcel Dzama's artwork.

4. [5] When Dzama was a twenty-one year old art student at the university of Winnipeg he helped start the renowned Royal art Lodge.

5. [3] In 2005 Dzama drew the album cover for Beck's record *Guero* he has also illustrated Nick Hornby's essay collection called Songbook.

6. [3] Many of Dzamas paintings feature the same elements nightmarish comic landscapes modern nostalgia, and bats.

7. [2] One of his most famous works a diorama of riflemen shooting down bats, birds, and severed heads shows Dzama's darkly comic sensibilities.

8. [4] Dzama described the meaning of his diorama "They're shooting the character's I decided I would'nt be drawing anymore".

9. [4] His artwork which has been exhibited at New York's museum of modern Art is popular among celebrities such as Jim Carrey.

10. [4] A best selling art book of Dzama's work, The Berlin years, was released in 2003, and Dzama co authored several other art collections.

11. [3] Adam Clay loves art "My mother always says, Art feeds the soul. "

12. [3] Adam, who speaks french puts art in his apartment near the Rideau canal.

UNIT Review

Answers may vary.

Add punctuation to the following sentences. If you don't know an answer, go back and review the appropriate section. Also underline three titles that should normally be italicized.

1. Most human's believe in life after death they want to believe that life has meaning.
2. My mother always says don't believe everything that you read.
3. Last month, I read the following The war of the worlds, 1984, and Animal farm.
4. In december, they celebrated thirty five years of marriage.
5. I read an article in The Boston Globe called The final shift.

Need more practice? Visit the Companion Website and try more grammar exercises.

Final Review

PART A

For each of the sentences, circle the letter of the answer that best fills in the blank. Note that *X* means "nothing."

1. Some people perform acts of kindness, including ___ donating time, money, and publicity to charities.
   a) ; b) : c) X
2. For the Diabetes Association, Alana donated the following ___ clothing, jewellery, and money.
   a) ; b) : c) X
3. She is self-sufficient ___ "I pay my own expenses ___
   a) : / "! b) , / !" c) : / !"
4. She loved the novel called ___
   a) "The Hunger Games"
   b) *The Hunger Games*
   c) *The hunger games*
5. The artist Paul Gauguin said ___ "Art is either plagiarism or revolution ___
   a) , / " (10). b) : / ." (10) c) : / " (10).

You can use the Final Review as a test. There are five answers in Part A and twenty-five in Part B for a total of twenty-five points. You can also find additional practice exercises and testing material on the Companion Website.

You can ask students to remove this page and hand it in. Note that in the student books, pages are perforated.

PART B

Identify five titles. Add quotation marks where appropriate and underline titles that should normally be italicized. Also correct fifteen other errors involving punctuation or capitalization.

6. Last september, an interesting article appeared in the Toronto Star. The article, called The art of Rewiring a Brain, describes artist John Newmans recovery from a stroke using art therapy. A journalist for the magazine Health News Digest also discusses the therapy.

7. In 2006, Newman's stroke took his lifes passion away from him he could no longer paint with his right hand. However, Newman taught himself to paint with his left hand. According to Newman, it was hard work, "I didn't have any control over my left hand." By the age of seventy eight, Newman's new artwork was again displayed in a prominent Toronto gallery. The exhibit lasted until friday, October 8.

8. Newman, a former professor at the Ontario College of Art and design believes that his brain made new connections when he constantly drew with his left hand. He thinks that other patient's can also use art therapy to help rebuild their brains.

9. An article in the Deccan herald entitled Healing Through Art showed that art therapy can also be useful for young people with emotional or psychological problems. Robert Allen, a visual art therapist, said: "it is a terrific diagnosis tool".

SPEAKING AND WRITING

Playing Paparazzi

Working with a partner, imagine a discussion between two well-known celebrities. Write ten lines of dialogue. Use quotation marks around direct speech.

Ask pairs of students to exchange their writing and peer edit for proper use of punctuation, capitalization, and use of quotations.

UNIT 12

Spelling and Word Choice

You can use the Preview activity to introduce spelling and word choice. Students can then complete the unit in class or for homework. Additional exercises appear on the Companion Website.

Preview

DICTATION

Your teacher will read nine sentences out loud. Write each of the sentences.

1. In schools, humans are taught how to win and lose gracefully.
2. I recommend that you try to fulfill your potential.
3. People should not be embarrassed about their successes or failures.
4. Their ninth child's height and weight were above average.
5. She exaggerates the amount of leisure time that she has.

6. The government minister appeared irresponsible.
7. He committed some errors when he addressed the crowd.
8. He definitely is a poor example for future generations.
9. My family has developed an efficient way to address problems.

Spelling: Forms and Usage

Spelling correctly is important. According to the Canadian Broadcasting Corporation, one spelling mistake on a commercial website can cut sales by half. Review the following spelling rules to help you become a better speller.

WRITING *–GHT* AND *–GTH*

The past forms of many verbs end in ***–ght***. In such words, the *–gh* is silent. Thus, *thought* is pronounced *thot*.

bou**ght**   cau**ght**

Other words end in ***–gth***. When you pronounce the following words, ensure that you pronounce the final *–th* by pushing your tongue slightly between your upper and lower front teeth.

stren**gth**   len**gth**

WRITING *–IE* OR *–EI*

To learn the spelling of words containing ***–ie*** or ***–ei***, remember the following rhyme. Write *–i* before *–e*, except after *–c*, or when *–ei* is pronounced as *ay*, as in *neighbour* and *weigh*.

***–i* before *–e*:**	bel**ie**ve	f**ie**ld
***–ei* after *–c*:**	re**cei**ve	**cei**ling
***–ei* pronounced as *ay*:**	w**ei**gh	v**ei**n

Note: There are several exceptions to the above rule.

an**cie**nt	for**ei**gn	l**ei**sure	s**cie**nce	so**cie**ty
either	h**ei**ght	n**ei**ther	s**ei**ze	w**ei**rd

ADDING PREFIXES AND SUFFIXES

A **prefix** is added to the beginning of a word, and it changes the word's meaning. When you add a prefix to a word, the last letter of the prefix and the first letter of the main word can be the same; keep both. Some common prefixes include *dis-*, *il-*, *im-*, *in-*, *mis-*, *non-*, and *re-*.

u**n** + **n**atural = u**nn**atural   mi**s** + **s**pell = mi**ss**pell

When you add a **suffix** to the end of a word, it changes the word's tense and/or meaning. When you add the suffix *–ly* to a root word that ends in *–l*, keep the *–l* of the root word. The new word will have two *–ls*. If the root word ends in *–e*, keep the *–e*.

fina**l** + **l**y = fina**ll**y   sur**e** + **l**y = sur**el**y

COMMONLY MISSPELLED WORDS

The following are some commonly misspelled words.

Note: A more complete list appears in *Avenues 3: Grammar Review Guide*.

address	embarrassed	government
aggressive	environment	heroes
apartment	exaggerated	human
bankrupt	example	interesting
committed	family	medicine
developed	future	ninth

➜

payment
personality
possess
potential
questioned
recommend
recommendation
responsibility
responsible
succeed
successful
tomorrow

Word Choice: Forms and Usage

The following sets of words sound alike but have very different meanings.

SOME COMMONLY CONFUSED WORDS

WORD	MEANING	USAGE
accept **except**	to receive; to admit excluding; other than	You should really **accept** my apology. Everyone **except** Lauren was at the movie.
allowed **aloud**	permitted spoken audibly	The children aren't **allowed** to stay up past nine. We couldn't speak **aloud**, so we whispered.
considerate **considered**	kind and understanding contemplated; regarded as	His lawyer was a very gentle and **considerate** person. He was **considered** the main suspect in the case.
hole **whole**	an opening in something the full amount	There is a large **hole** where the house used to be. The company tore down the **whole** house.
independence **independent**	the state of being free from control not controlled by others	India celebrated fifty years of **independence**. Katia is **independent**. She pays her own bills.
loose **lose** **loss** **lost**	not tight; baggy to misplace something a decrease in value misplaced or unable to be found; unable to find one's way (past form of *lose*)	My pants are too **loose**. I need a belt. I often **lose** my keys. The company suffered a **loss** for the third year in a row. We didn't know how to get to the new store, and instead we got **lost**.
price **prize**	the cost of something a reward for winning a contest	The sofa is on sale for a very good **price**. He won the contest, and his **prize** was a trip to Hawaii.
quiet **quit** **quite**	silent to discontinue a job or habit to a considerable degree	It is very **quiet** outside. There are no sounds. Marco **quit** smoking. He also **quit** his job. The politician is **quite** young. He's just twenty years old.
sale **sell**	a reduced price to transfer something in exchange for money	The tires were on **sale** for fifty percent off. The new hardware store **sells** tires.
steal **still**	to take without permission remaining in place; a past situation continues to exist	The thief tried to **steal** my car. The thief is sitting very **still** in his cell. He is **still** in police custody.

Practice

EXERCISE 1 **IDENTIFY SPELLING ERRORS**

Underline and correct sixteen spelling mistakes in the following paragraphs. You could review the list of commonly misspelled words on pages 132–133.

fight
EXAMPLE: People want a better world so they figth for justice.

1. For a democracy to suceed [succeed], citizens must be able to speak freely about issues. A SLAPP, or strategic lawsuit against public participation, permits someone to act in an agressive [aggressive] manner toward critics. Unfortunatly [Unfortunately], private citizens have very little protection against such lawsuits.

2. Often, SLAPP cases relate to the enviroment [environment]. For exemple [example], in 2004, Serge Galipeau and Christine Landry complained about the strong odours from a nearby dump. They couldn't leave the windows of their appartement [apartment] open because they developped [developed] headaches. The dump's owners, who were embarased [embarrassed] by the publicity, brought a $1.25 million defamation lawsuit against the couple. Any business owner with a deceitful personnality [personality] may exagerrate [exaggerate] the damage to the company's reputation. However, it is unnethical [unethical] to allow companies to silence consumers.

3. To discourage any futur [future] SLAPPs, some governments have introduced anti-SLAPP legislation. For example, Quebec and Pennsylvania have such laws. Hopefully, companies will take responsability [responsibility] for their mistakes instead of attacking critics. However, many people have questionned [questioned] the effectiveness of anti-SLAPP legislation. Meanwhile, many victims of SLAPPs spend a lot of time and money defending themselves. They are not always successfull [successful]. Still, most whistle-blowers recommand [recommend] that people fight for justice.

SPELLING TWO-PART WORDS

Some indefinite pronouns sound as if they should be two separate words, but they are only one.

- **Words with *any*:** anything, anyone, anybody, anywhere
- **Words with *some*:** something, someone, somebody, somewhere
- **Words with *every*:** everything, everyone, everybody, everywhere

Another* and *A lot

Another is always one word. Bonnie committed **another** crime.

A lot is always two words. She robbed **a lot** of banks.

TIP

Words Ending in *–ful*

Although the word *full* ends in two *–ls*, when *full* is added to another word as a suffix, it ends in only one *–l*.

beautifu**l** peacefu**l** wonderfu**l**

Exception: Notice the unusual spelling when *full* and *fill* are combined: *fulfill*.

Note: When you add the suffix *–ly*, the final word has two *–ls*.

beautifu**ll**y peacefu**ll**y wonderfu**ll**y

EXERCISE 2 **IDENTIFY SPELLING ERRORS**

Underline and correct fifteen spelling mistakes.

Another
EXAMPLE: An other scandal occurred last year.

1. Many good people enter politics because they believe it is a fullfilling [fulfilling] job. They are truthfull [truthful], and they have the personal strenght [strength] to avoid making imoral [immoral] choices. However, not all politicians are honest. Some times [Sometimes] they accept bribes. Alot [A lot] of political leaders have definitly [definitely] been involved in scandals. In 1995, Canadian Prime Minister Brian Mulroney was accused of accepting a $225,000 cash paiement [payment] placed in an envelope, but he said it was for work he had done.

2. In addition, during Canada's 2011 election, some body [somebody] orchestrated "robocalls" to voters, telling them to go to an other [another] polling station. Voters turned up at the new locations and realized that the calls had been a hoax. →

Often, when they finaly [finally] made it to the real polling stations, they were too late and couldn't vote. No body [Nobody] knows who organized the calls. Often, citizens discover that their heros [heroes], especially in the governement [government], are capable of just about any thing [anything].

STANDARD ENGLISH

In both academic and professional writing, you should use standard English. The word *standard* doesn't imply "better." Standard English is the common language generally used and expected in schools, businesses, and government institutions.

Avoid Slang

Slang is non-standard language that is used in informal situations. In academic writing, it is preferable to use more formal terms. Review the following examples of slang.

cool guy dude kid psyched stuff

Slang: The kid was psyched.
Better: The **child** was **excited**.

TIP

Changing Slang

Slang changes over time, and it also differs depending on generational and regional influences. For example, in the past, people used the words *swell* or *groovy* to show admiration. More recent terms are *awesome*, *cool*, and *sick*. In fact, very soon, some of this book's examples might be considered "lame."

Ask students to do Exercise 3 with a partner. If students don't know the meaning of *TLC*, explain to them that it means "tender loving care."

EXERCISE 3 **IDENTIFY SLANG**

Underline and correct ten examples of slang. Replace each slang term with a standard English word.

EXAMPLE: The old dude [man] was really surprised.

Answers will vary.

1. Philip Zimbardo, a psychology professor, wanted to determine if roles make people behave badly. In the Stanford Prison Experiment, some regular guys [men] agreed to play the role of prisoners, and others played the role of prison guards. The prisoners weren't allowed to bring any of their personal stuff [belongings] into the simulated prison.

2. Originally, Zimbardo thought the guards would show some TLC to the prisoners, but he was really shocked when some of the guards started acting like total jerks. They did some bad stuff to the prisoners.

3. One of the guards, for instance, was totally not cool. He became full of it, and he started making rules that were dumb. The men who were the prisoners became really whipped. A few of them freaked and left the experiment early.

TIP

Rob and *Steal*

Both ***rob*** and ***steal*** mean "to take property illegally." However, *to steal* is to take an entire object. *To rob* is to take something from the object or to take something from someone. Notice the difference in meaning.

He **robbed** the car.	He took valuables, such as the GPS device, from the car.
He **robbed** me.	He took something from me.
He **stole** the car.	He took the car.

EXERCISE 4 **WORD CHOICE**

Underline the appropriate word in parentheses. If you are not sure of your answer, review the list of commonly confused words on page 133.

EXAMPLE: What have you got to (loose / lose)? Take a chance!

1. In my family, everyone (accept / except) my mother is interested in politics. We have spent (hole / whole) weekends debating issues. My father hates to (loose / loss / lose) the debates, so he uses persuasive tactics to convince us that he is right. He is never at a (lose / loss / lost) for words. My mother, on the other hand, remains (quit / quite / quiet). During our discussions, we are (considered / considerate) to each other. For instance, last weekend, we discussed non-violent revolutions. Five days later, we are (steal / still) discussing the topic.

2. Most people (accept / except) that non-violent revolution is possible. In fact, non-violent resistance has (aloud / allowed) many nations to emerge from authoritarianism. For example, the Singing Revolution in Eastern Europe led to Estonia, Latvia, and Lithuania gaining (independents / independence). Even →

better, those countries won their freedom without paying a heavy (prize / price) in lives (loss / lost). During the Singing Revolution, hundreds of thousands of people sang their national anthems, which was a right they had (lose / lost / loss) during Soviet rule. They were really (quit / quite / quiet) brave, because they often faced Soviet tanks. They were tired of Soviet authorities (stealing / robbing) them. After four years of civil disobedience, those countries finally won the (prize / price) of freedom, in 1991.

3. Democratic governments can help people who are living under dictatorships. For instance, trade embargoes have been effective. Often, a group of countries refuses to (sale / sell) weapons to the authoritarian regime. People in privileged nations should be (considered / considerate) and try to help where they can. For example, 2010 saw the growth of the "Arab Spring." Many people (considered / considerate) certain Middle Eastern dictators untouchable just a few short years ago, but people in Tunisia and Egypt have proven the power of non-violent resistance.

MORE COMMONLY CONFUSED WORDS

Some English words may look like words in your own language. However, their meaning in English may not match their meaning in your language. Memorize the following words and their meanings.

Learn* and *Teach

A person discovering information ***learns***. A person providing information ***teaches***.

He **learned** how to read when he was five.
His mother **taught** him how to read.

Memory*, *Remind*, *Remember*, and *Souvenir

Memory is a noun meaning "the capacity to retain past impressions." ***Remind*** is a verb meaning "to cause a person to remember something." ***Remember*** is a verb meaning "to recall." A ***souvenir*** is a memento that you buy to remind yourself of a special place.

When we went to New York, we brought back a **souvenir** of the Statue of Liberty. I **remember** many details about our trip. Please **remind** me to call my grandmother and tell her about it. She is eighty, but she has a great **memory**.

Say* and *Tell

Use ***say*** in direct and indirect quotations. Follow *say* with the actual words that were said. ***Tell*** is followed by a noun or pronoun. You must tell somebody something.

Alex **said**, "Let's move to Nova Scotia."
He **told** me that he wanted to move to Halifax.

TIP

Quit

You do not quit a person or place, you leave it.

He ~~quit~~ **left** the country last month.

EXERCISE 5 **MORE WORD CHOICE**

Underline and correct one error involving commonly confused words in each of the sentences below. Write *C* beside the sentences that are correct.

1. Some soldiers loose [lose] the ability to cope with everyday life after they leave the battlefield. ______ A psychology professor learned [taught] me the about the symptoms and effects of post-traumatic stress disorder (PTSD). ______ He said [told] me that soldiers in war zones are especially susceptible to developing PTSD. ______ About 12 percent of veterans develop the disorder after they are exposed to high-risk combat situations. __C__ For instance, my professor said that if I spent a hole [whole] year on the front lines in Iraq, I would have a chance of developing it. ______

2. For many soldiers, quitting [leaving] a war zone and returning home is traumatic. ______ Often, family members feel like the PTSD has stolen [robbed] them of the person they used to know. ______ For instance, some veterans from the Afghanistan conflict aloud [allowed] psychologists to question them. ______ The former soldiers said that certain events can remember [remind] them of their war experiences, a phenomenon known as "flashbacks." ______ Even thirty years later, many retain painful souvenirs [memories] of the war. ______ Some soldiers loose [lose] their moral balance. ______ For example, a veteran living in New York shot a neighbour because he thought the man was an intruder. __C__ He said, "I thought he stole [robbed] me and was going to take my computer!" ______

3. Studies on soldiers should learn [teach] us about the importance of providing psychological assistance to those returning from combat. ______ It's important not to glorify wars or diminish the impact they have on the soldiers who fight them. __C__ It was Oscar Wilde who told [said], "As long as war is regarded as wicked, it will always have its fascination. ______ When it is looked upon as vulgar, it will cease to be popular." __C__

PREPOSITIONAL EXPRESSIONS

Some words are followed by certain prepositions. Memorize the following **prepositional expressions** and the two examples of their usage. A more complete list of prepositional expressions appears in your *Avenues 3: Grammar Review Guide*.

apologize for	consist of	look at	responsible for
ask for	depend on	participate in	scared of
believe in	insist on	prepared for	search for
capable of	interested in	rely on	specialize in

Toni was responsible **for** the accident.

They depend **on** science to answer difficult questions.

EXERCISE 6 **PREPOSITIONAL EXPRESSIONS**

Fill in the blanks with appropriate prepositions to complete the prepositional expressions.

EXAMPLE: My father really depends _on_ my mother.

1. In times of need, can we depend ___on___ others to help us? A part of the brain, called the limbic system, is responsible ___for___ our emotional reactions. In the past, some scientists believed that humans were not capable ___of___ altruistic behaviour until they were properly socialized and their brains were fairly developed. However, some intriguing studies suggest that helpful behaviour begins at a very early age.

2. Felix Warneken and Mike Tomasello are researchers who specialize ___in___ human behaviour, and they are interested ___in___ altruism. They developed scenarios in which an adult wasn't capable ___of___ solving a simple problem. Some very young children participated ___in___ the experiments. In one study, Warneken hung clothing on a line and then dropped a peg that was out of his reach while a baby played nearby. He looked ___at___ the baby, but he didn't ask ___for___ help. Over 80 percent of the time, the baby would pick up the peg and hand it to him.

3. In another version of the experiment, Warneken threw the peg on the ground. In those tests, the babies appeared to be scared ___of___ him, and they didn't pick up the item. The babies helped Warneken only when they knew that he needed help to complete his goal of hanging the clothes.

4. The experiments indicate that infants, who have very little socialization or language skills, are willing to help others. They feel responsible __for__ the well-being of people around them. Such studies help explain why human beings can rely __on__ each other in times of need.

UNIT Review

Complete the following exercises. If you don't know an answer, go back and review the appropriate section.

1. Underline the correctly spelled words in the pairs below.
   - a) nineth / ninth
   - b) fulfil / fulfill
   - c) naturally / naturaly
   - d) adress / address
   - e) responsible / responsable
   - f) government / governement
2. Underline and correct the word-usage errors in the sentences below.
   - a) You might win a price (prize) if you buy a ticket for the contest.
   - b) My coach said (told) me to work harder.
   - c) I need to sale (sell) some of my old hockey equipment.
   - d) Tony is responsible of (for) the boy's death.

COMPANION WEB+ Need more practice? Visit the Companion Website and try additional grammar exercises.

Final Review

You can use the Final Review as a test. There are twelve answers in Part A and eight answers in Part B for a total of twenty points. You can also find additional practice exercises and testing material on the Companion Website.

PART A

Correct all misspelled words from the following list. Write *C* next to the words that are spelled correctly.

EXAMPLE: shure __sure__

1. unusualy	unusually	**7.** recommand	recommend
2. writting	writing	**8.** another	C
3. exaggerated	C	**9.** alot	a lot
4. personnality	personality	**10.** questionning	questioning
5. responsability	responsibility	**11.** definitly	definitely
6. strenght	strength	**12.** finally	C

PART B

Underline and correct eight errors involving word choice.

taught
EXAMPLE: My father <u>learned</u> me about the case.

13. What moves people to action? Recently, somebody
reminded
<u>remembered</u> me of an article by Nicholas Kristof called "What Moves Us." He explains that good people aren't moved by news about genocide and famine. However, if someone
loses
<u>looses</u> a child or a puppy, humans react. In one experiment, psychologists asked people to give $5 to charity. They were
allowed
<u>aloud</u> to choose who would get the money: a seven-year-old girl or 21 million Africans. For most participants, the young
considered
girl was <u>considerate</u> the most deserving of the money. Kristof
says
<u>tells</u>, "Evidence is overwhelming that humans respond to the suffering of individuals rather than groups."

You can ask students to remove this page and hand it in. Note that in the student books, pages are perforated.

accept
14. If we <u>except</u> the research, what does this mean for charities? If an animal
sell
shelter wants to <u>sale</u> charity tickets to raise money, it should mention a
teach
specific dog in its publicity. Perhaps Kristof should <u>learn</u> aid organizations about the study.

SPEAKING AND WRITING

Ask students to exchange their writing and peer edit for proper spelling and for use of commonly confused words.

Identify Your Misspelled Words

Working with a partner, review the commonly misspelled words in your *Avenues 3: Grammar Review Guide*. Using your partner's booklet, quiz him or her on words. Underline or highlight every word that your partner misspells. Then give your review guide to your partner, and he or she will quiz you.

When you finish, construct a paragraph using some of the words that you commonly misspell.

Editing Practice and Tense Review

Note that editing symbols are added to exercises 1 and 2 so that students can practise editing using those symbols.

Practise editing student writing. The following exercises contain a variety of errors.

EXERCISE 1 **EDITING**

Correct twenty-five errors in this student essay, not including the example. An editing symbol appears above each error. To understand the meaning of each symbol, look at the "Guide for Correcting Writing Errors" on the inside back cover of this book.

~~the~~ (X) they (WC)

1. What is <u>the</u> beauty? Some people think that <u>you</u> need a perfect body. They are

influenced (WF)

<u>influence</u> by the media and the photos of famous people who are beautiful.

those (PL)

But <u>that</u> celebrities sometimes have surgery to look perfect. In addition,

Unfortunately (SP)

photographers retouch pictures of famous people. <u>Unfortunatly</u>, people take

dangerous risks to attain a beauty ideal.

don't eat (VT) their (WC)

2. First, some people <u>are not eating</u> very much and it affects <u>her</u> health

example (SP) ~~she~~ (DS) always tries (VT) lose (WC)

For <u>exemple</u>, my friend <u>she</u> <u>is always trying</u> to <u>loose</u> weight, and she doesn't

~~like~~ (X) went (VT)

look <u>like</u> very good. Last year, she <u>was going</u> to the hospital three times.

We worried about her. Today, she still has an eating disorder.

things
PL
3. Men also do horrible thing to be perfect in the eyes of society. One of the biggest

problems PL drugs PL
problem for men is steroids. Those drug are easy to get. Steroids can cause many

health SP exercise VT
problems for men's healt. Sometimes, men also are exercising for hours each day.

each day because F Spanish C
Because they want to be muscular. My friend, who speaks spanish, goes to the

gym every day. He thinks his muscles will impress women. But sometimes he

himself SP has had VT with SP
pushes hisself too much. Since last April, he has many problems wiht his knees.

4. Every day, people do dangerous things to look perfect. Instead, they should try

the beauty ideal be WO
to enjoy life and not worry about their appearance. What will be the beauty ideal

future SP
in the futur? Maybe women of average size and men with very little muscle

considered WC
development will be considerate perfect.

EXERCISE 2 EDITING

Correct twenty errors in in the following student paragraph. An editing symbol appears above each error. To understand the meaning of each symbol, look at the "Guide for Correcting Writing Errors" on the inside back cover of this book.

experienced WC literature SP
Almost everyone has experimented the magic of litterature. Writers share

points PL think WF
personal point of view. Essays and stories make us thinking about issues in our

Additionally SP hearing WF
society. Additionaly, most of us enjoy to hear about the past. For example, in the

Visit C readers/us ⬭ Canadian C
text "My visit to Montreal," Susanna Moodie tells ^ about that canadian city in the

understand WF she was WO
1830s. Her story helps us understands what was she feeling at that time. Her

were ;
SV RO
impressions of Montreal was mixed, she thought that the scenery was beautiful,

people the streets were dirty
PL //
the persons were friendly, and there were dirty streets. She describes the smells

: " (119).
P P
in the city, "The air was loaded with intolerable vapours". (119) She also tells

who
WC
a story about a man which drowned because bystanders didn't help him. She

~~do~~
X
questions why do people ignore others who are in distress. Definitely, reading

another
⌒
can teach us about an other time and place.

EXERCISE 3 TENSE PROBLEMS

Underline and correct fifteen errors. Look for problems with verb tense and spelling, as well as errors with modals and conditional forms.

1. In 2006, Microsoft dominated the personal-computer market. To get a larger

market share, Apple launched a clever ad campaign. The "Get a Mac"

~~has~~ would
campaign has lasted from 2006 to 2010. In each ad, a young, hip guy will say,

reply
"I'm a Mac." An older man in a suit would replied, "I'm a PC." Each commercial

had a little story. For example, in the first commercial, the PC complained about

mentioned
the viruses that could affect him. The Mac quietly mentionned that he did not get

would remain
viruses. In every ad, the PC will get agitated, and the Mac would remaining calm.

feel
2. The ads were extremely successful, but they also made Bill Gates feeling quite

had
angry. Perhaps if Microsoft would have spent more money on better advertising,

responded could
it could have responded effectively. At that time, most consumers can see the

laughed
humour in the ads, and they laught at Microsoft. The ads were very effective.

have
In fact, since the ads first aired, many consumers ^ switched from PC computers

thought
to Apple computers. However, back in 2006, some consumers thougth that

were
the commercials was unfair. That year, in an article for *Slate* magazine,

~~has~~
Seth Stevenson has wrote that the ads were "mean-spirited."

EXERCISE 4 **EDITING**

Underline and correct twenty grammar errors.

1. Memory plays an important role in ours [our] lives. But would the ability to remember every detail being [be] useful? Actress Marilu Henner has a condition called "highly superior autobiographical memory." During her childhood, she has [~~has~~] discovered that she could remember details about each days [day]. If Henner would have [had] become a professor or other academic, she probably would of [have] realized the rarity of her condition. Certainly, her amazing memory has been very helpful in her career as an actress.

2. Next month, I'm gonna [going to] get married to a man named Jonas. I wish that he has [had] a better memory. He is a forty-years [year]-old man, and his memory is worst [worse] than it used to be. He can not [cannot / can't] remember details about the past, and its [it's] annoying. To illustrate, I'll describe an incident in our lives. Last month him [he] and me [I] had a huge argument about our wedding. Him [He] and his brother wanted to wear jeans to the wedding, but I disagreed with theirs [their] plans. Today, Jonas claims that the argument didn't happened [happen] and he had never mention [mentioned] jeans. I wish I [had] recorded the conversation last month. Perhaps by the time we get married, we will forget [have forgotten] the argument.

EXERCISE 5 **"HOW" QUESTIONS**

Complete each of the following questions by adding one of the missing words below:

far   long   many   much   often   old

EXAMPLE: How _much_ is that coat? Is it $15?

1. How ____old____ is Jamie? Is she twenty years old?
2. How ____often____ do you visit a doctor? Do you go twice a year?
3. How ____long____ is the movie: two or three hours?
4. How ____many____ people are in the lineup? Are there a lot of people?
5. How ____far____ is Winnipeg? Is it more than 200 kilometres from here?
6. How ____old____ was Tania when she moved away? Was she sixteen years old?

7. How ___long___ have you been in college? Have you been here for one or two years?

8. How ___much___ is that house? Does it cost more than $300,000?

9. How ___often___ do you travel: once or twice a year?

EXERCISE 6 QUESTIONS

Students wrote questions about the article "Memories of 9/11" on page 12 of *Avenues 3: English Skills*. Identify and correct the errors in each of the following sentences.

EXAMPLE: Where ^does Brian Clark live?

1. When he started (did he start) to work at the World Trade Center?

2. Why ^(were) his colleagues ~~were~~ afraid?

3. How ~~much~~ long did Clark stay inside the burning building?

4. Since 2001, how many times ^(has) ~~did~~ Clark visited New York?

5. Where he is (is he) living now?

6. What he did (did he do) when the plane hit the building?

7. How long ~~time~~ did Stanley Praimnath spend under the desk?

8. In the future, what will ~~be~~ the reaction to a terrorist attack ^(be)?

Ask students to do Exercise 7 in teams. You can make this a timed competition.

EXERCISE 7 FIVE KEY RULES

In this exercise, errors represent some major grammar problems. Errors are indicated in bold. Correct each error, then write a rule for each correction.

1. Everyone **have** (has) problems. For example, my friend **want** (wants) a better job.

Rule: In the present, add *-s* or *-es* to verbs that follow third-person-singular subjects.

See Unit 1 for more information about subject-verb agreement.

2. Since Dylan graduated, he **work** (has worked) in advertising. He **made** (has made) many anti-drug commercials. He says that **he never took** (has never taken) drugs in his life.

Rule: Use the present perfect tense when a past action continues to the present moment or when an action occurred at unknown past times.

See Unit 3 for more information about present perfect tenses.

easily

3. Children can learn languages more **easier** than adults can. Their brains can

more quickly

absorb new information **quicker** than adult brains can.

Rule: Many adverbs end in *–ly*, thus you must retain the adverb form in a comparison.

See Unit 5 for more information about adverbs.

specific / their / year

4. Mira and Samuel have **specifics** concerns about **theirs** ten-**years**-old son David.

Rule: Adjectives are never plural.

See Unit 5, page 53, for more information about adjectives and Unit 8, page 77, for more information about plurals.

have

5. When the plane hit the building, Brian Clark should **of** left immediately.

have

His colleagues should **of** gone downstairs instead of upstairs.

Rule: With past forms of the modals *should*, *could*, and *would*, use *have* + past participle.

See Unit 6 for more information about modal forms.

had

6. Last May, my grandfather died. If I **would have** known that he was ill, I would have spent more time with him.

Rule: In past conditional sentences, use the past perfect tense in *if* clauses.

See Unit 7 for more information about conditional sentences.

. It's

7. People love to travel, **it's** a passion for them. They travel to practise using new

;

languages, they also learn about different ways of thinking.

Rule: Do not join two complete ideas with a comma.

See Unit 10 for more information about combining sentences.

, / will" (124).

8. Jan Wong said; "My God forgive me; I don't think they every will." **(124)**

Rule: In quotations, put a comma after an opening phrase and the final period after the page number.

See Unit 11 for more information about punctuation.

Irregular Verb List

The following list has three columns:

- The **base form** appears in dictionaries. Use the base form in the present tense after auxiliaries such as *do*, *did*, *does*, *can*, and *should*, and after *to* in infinitives.

  EXAMPLE: You didn't help.

- Use the **simple past** form with the simple past tense.

  EXAMPLE: We bought a ticket yesterday.

- Use the **past participle** form in perfect and passive structures.

  EXAMPLE: She has been to England three times.

BASE FORM	SIMPLE PAST	PAST PARTICIPLE	BASE FORM	SIMPLE PAST	PAST PARTICIPLE
be	was/were	been	**do**	did	done
beat	beat	beat/beaten	**draw**	drew	drawn
become	became	become	**drink**	drank	drunk
begin	began	begun	**drive**	drove	driven
bend	bent	bent	**eat**	ate	eaten
bet	bet	bet	**fall**	fell	fallen
bind	bound	bound	**feed**	fed	fed
bite	bit	bitten	**feel**	felt	felt
bleed	bled	bled	**fight**	fought	fought
blow	blew	blown	**find**	found	found
break	broke	broken	**fit**	fit	fit
breed	bred	bred	**flee**	fled	fled
bring	brought	brought	**fly**	flew	flown
build	built	built	**forbid**	forbade	forbidden
burst	burst	burst	**foresee**	foresaw	foreseen
buy	bought	bought	**forget**	forgot	forgotten
catch	caught	caught	**forgive**	forgave	forgiven
choose	chose	chosen	**freeze**	froze	frozen
cling	clung	clung	**get**	got	got/gotten
come	came	come	**give**	gave	given
cost	cost	cost	**go**	went	gone
creep	crept	crept	**grind**	ground	ground
cut	cut	cut	**grow**	grew	grown
deal	dealt	dealt	**hang**[1]	hung	hung
dig	dug	dug	**have**	had	had

1. When *hang* means "to suspend by a rope, as in a form of capital punishment," then it is a **regular verb**. The past forms are *hanged*.

BASE FORM	SIMPLE PAST	PAST PARTICIPLE	BASE FORM	SIMPLE PAST	PAST PARTICIPLE
hear	heard	heard	**shrink**	shrank	shrunk
hide	hid	hidden	**shut**	shut	shut
hit	hit	hit	**sing**	sang	sung
hold	held	held	**sink**	sank	sunk
hurt	hurt	hurt	**sit**	sat	sat
keep	kept	kept	**sleep**	slept	slept
kneel	knelt/kneeled	knelt/kneeled	**slide**	slid	slid
know	knew	known	**speak**	spoke	spoken
lay	laid	laid	**speed**	sped	sped
lead	led	led	**spend**	spent	spent
leave	left	left	**spin**	spun	spun
lend	lent	lent	**split**	split	split
let	let	let	**spread**	spread	spread
lie[2]	lay	lain	**stand**	stood	stood
light	lit	lit	**steal**	stole	stolen
lose	lost	lost	**stick**	stuck	stuck
make	made	made	**sting**	stung	stung
mean	meant	meant	**stink**	stank	stunk
meet	met	met	**strike**	struck	struck
mislead	misled	misled	**strive**	strove	striven
mistake	mistook	mistaken	**swear**	swore	sworn
pay	paid	paid	**sweep**	swept	swept
prove	proved	proved/proven	**swim**	swam	swum
put	put	put	**swing**	swung	swung
quit	quit	quit	**take**	took	taken
read[3]	read	read	**teach**	taught	taught
ride	rode	ridden	**tear**	tore	torn
ring	rang	rung	**tell**	told	told
rise	rose	risen	**think**	thought	thought
run	ran	run	**throw**	threw	thrown
say	said	said	**thrust**	thrust	thrust
see	saw	seen	**understand**	understood	understood
sell	sold	sold	**upset**	upset	upset
send	sent	sent	**wake**	woke	woken
set	set	set	**wear**	wore	worn
shake	shook	shaken	**win**	won	won
shoot	shot	shot	**withdraw**	withdrew	withdrawn
show	showed	shown	**write**	wrote	written

2. *Lie* means "to rest or lie down, such as on a sofa or bed." When *lie* means "to tell a false statement," it is a regular verb: *lie–lied–lied*.
3. The present form of *read* is pronounced "reed." The simple past and past participle forms are pronounced "red."

Parts of Speech

PART OF SPEECH	DEFINITION	EXAMPLES
adjective	Adds information about the noun.	small, hot, beautiful, green
adverb	Adds information about the verb. Expresses time, place, or frequency.	easily, nicely, quickly, quietly sometimes, usually, often, never
conjunction	Connects two parts of a sentence. • **coordinating:** Connects two ideas of equal importance. • **subordinating:** Connects a subordinate (or secondary) idea to the main idea.	 and, but, so, or after, although, because, unless
determiner	Identifies or determines if the noun is specific or general.	a, an, the, this, that, these, those, each, every, much, many, some
noun (common)	Person, place or thing.	**Singular:** woman, cat, person **Plural:** women, cats, people
noun (proper)	Specific person, place or thing. Proper nouns are capitalized.	Jamaica, Doctor Reed, Samson, Lake Ontario, Golden Gate Bridge, Calgary
preposition	Shows a relationship between words (source, direction, location, etc.).	above, at, behind, below, for, from, of, to
pronoun	Replaces the noun.	he, she, it, us, ours, themselves
verb	Expresses an action or state.	talk, walk, think, drive

PRACTICE

Label each word with one of the following terms.

adjective conjunction noun (common) pronoun verb
adverb determiner noun (proper) preposition

EXAMPLE: clear Adjective

1. herself pronoun
2. and conjunction
3. human noun (common)
4. develop verb
5. under preposition
6. blue adjective
7. often adverb
8. into preposition
9. theirs pronoun
10. break verb
11. children noun (common)
12. easily adverb
13. the determiner
14. Mrs. Grey noun (proper)

Combining Ideas in Sentences

MAKING COMPOUND SENTENCES

A.

Complete idea | **, coordinator** | complete idea

, but
, or
, yet
, so
, for
, and
, nor

B.

Complete idea **;** complete idea

C.

Complete idea | **; transitional expression,** | complete idea

; however,
; in fact,
; moreover,
; therefore,
; furthermore,

MAKING COMPLEX SENTENCES

D.

Complete idea | **subordinator** | incomplete idea

although
because
before
even though
unless
when

E. **Subordinator** | incomplete idea **,** complete idea

Although
Because
Before
Even though
Unless
When

APPENDIX 4

Spelling and Grammar Logs

In the first few pages of your writing portfolio or copybook, try keeping two logs to help you avoid repeating errors and to improve your writing.

SPELLING LOG

The goal of keeping a spelling log is to stop repeating errors. Every time you misspell a word, record both the mistake and the correction in your spelling log. Then, before you hand in a writing assignment, consult your list of misspelled words to ensure you're not repeating past errors.

Incorrect	Correct
finaly	finally
responsable	responsible

GRAMMAR LOG

The goal of keeping a grammar log is to stop repeating errors in sentence structure, mechanics, and punctuation. Each time a writing assignment is returned to you, identify one or two repeated grammar errors and add them to your grammar log. Next, consult the grammar log before you hand in new writing assignments in order to avoid making the same errors. For each type of grammar error, you could do the following:

1. Identify the assignment and write down the type of error.
2. In your own words, write a rule about the error.
3. Include an example from your writing assignment.

    1. Descriptive paragraph (Mar. 10) Fragment
    2. Sentences must have a subject and verb and express a complete thought.
    3. Also, my fears. ~~They~~ were irrational.

Spelling Log

Grammar Log

INDEX

PHOTO CREDITS

ALAMY
p. 9 © MARKA; p. 12 bottom, left © J. Sutton-Hibbert; p. 19 © Trinity Mirror/Mirropix; p. 30 © Pictorial Press Ltd.; p. 69 © Mandoga Media; pp. 70, 83 © ZUMA Wire Service; p. 82 © EIGHTFISH; p. 112 © EPA; p. 113 © arindambanerjee; p. 114 © Monkey Business Images; p. 124 © J. Sutton-Hibbert.

GAETZ, LYNNE: pp. 117, 129 top.

ISTOCKPHOTO: p. 18 © P. Wei; p. 32 © J. Bryson.

NATIONAL TRAFFIC SAFETY BOARD, USA: p. 40.

SHUTTERSTOCK
pp. 1 top, 10 top, 61 © S. Anna; p. 1 bottom © L. Smokovski; p. 3 © E. Durov; p. 4 © mmarcol; p. 5 © kaczor58; p. 7 top: © GlobetrotterJ; bottom: © irabel8; pp. 8, 105 © lynea; p. 10 bottom © Scenic Shutterbug; p. 11 © topten22photo; pp. 12 top, 24 © ifong; p. 12 bottom, right © Pinkcandy; p. 16 © holbox; p. 17 © B. Werkmann; p. 21 top: © Lisa S.; bottom: © J. Sharp; p. 22 © N. Tsvetkov; p. 24 bottom © ssguy; p. 25 © C. E. Santa-Maria; pp. 26 top, 36 top © T. Irina; pp. 26 middle, 57 middle, 109 © a. m. piacquadio; p. 28 © Contessa; p. 29 top: © A. Bayda; bottom: © nito; p. 31 © p. Michalis; p. 33 © elena1110; p. 34 bottom © D. Howell; p. 35 © beemanja; p. 36 bottom © H. Esteb; p. 37 © catwalker; pp. 38 top, 44 top © B. Rolff; p. 38 middle © K. R. Solana; p. 41 © L. Vandoorne; p. 42 © Seet; p. 43 © Blend Images; p. 44 bottom © Pius Lee; pp. 46 top, 55 top © A. Nekrassov; p. 48 © A. Muzika; p. 49 © I. Andriyanov; p. 50 © S. Duda; p. 51 © discpicture; p. 52 © D. Heinemann; p. 53 © t. sayig; p. 54 © Blueminiu; p. 55 middle © W. Muenzker; p. 56 © thieury; pp. 57 top, 64 top and bottom © U. Zunic; p. 59 top: © D. Sabljack; bottom: © JeniFoto; p. 60 © mtkang; p. 62 © J. Kershner; p. 63 © wavebreakmedia; p. 65 © A. Raths; pp. 66 top, 74 middle © italianestro; p. 66 middle © D. Beeler; p. 67 © photobank ch; p. 68 top: © Dhoxax; bottom: © Kom; p. 71 © D. Flowers; p. 72 © J. Wendler; p. 73 © haak78; p. 74 middle © dutourdumonde; p. 75 © bloomua; pp. 76 top, 88 top © A. Prado Photo; p. 76 middle © N. Vishneveckiy; p. 80 © sgm; p. 81 © pcruciatti; p. 84 © Citylights; p. 86 © C. Harvey; pp. 87, 139 © F. Mizioznikov; p. 88 bottom © arindambanerjee; p. 89 © Padmayogini; pp. 90 top, 100 top, 106 © Lightspring; p. 90 bottom © C. Brutiag; p. 92 © M. Gobson; p. 93 © Dariush M.; p. 94 © justasc; p. 96 © Elnur; p. 97 © V.P.; p. 98 © kathmanduphotog; p. 100 middle © Tracing Tea; pp. 102 top, 115 top © S. Tucker; p. 102 middle © R. Bayer; p. 107 © Elsayyed; p. 110 © Pixachi; p. 111 © V. Smirnov; p. 116 © L. Martin; p. 117 bottom © g. yim; p. 120 © M. Blinkov; p. 121 © A. castelli; p. 123 © Nyuuness; p. 125 © bogdanhoda; p. 127 © silver-john; p. 128 © Danicak; p. 129 bottom © Neftali; p. 130 © V. Wrangel; pp. 131 top, 141 top © Djsash; p. 131 bottom © J. Krcmar; p. 134 © dream designs; p. 135 © Lisa B.; p. 137 © F. Gregory; p. 138 © Shutterwolf; p. 140 © V. Trofer; p. 142 © Ossile.

THINKSTOCK: p. 31.